VITAL SIGNS
New and Selected Poems

VITAL SIGNS

New and
Selected Poems

DAVID R. SLAVITT

1975

DOUBLEDAY & COMPANY, INC.

GARDEN CITY, NEW YORK

DRAWINGS BY RAYMOND DAVIDSON

The author gratefully acknowledges the editors of the following magazines where several of the new poems originally appeared: "Letter to My Son, at School" and "After Catullus" in the *New Orleans Review*. Copyright © 1973 by Loyola University, New Orleans. Reprinted by permission of the *New Orleans Review*, "Tanagers," "Hatred," and "Cruising" in *The Yale Review*. Copyright Yale University; "The Complaint of Theodore Prodromos" in *The Andover Review*; "The Calf and the Ox" in YES (A Magazine of Poetry). Copyright © 1973 by Virginia Elson and Beverlee Hughes.

The following poems have appeared in previously published books: "Lepidopteran," "Partiti da Cotesti Che Son Morti," "Solomon Grundy," "Balloons," "Blocks," "Actaeon," "Orpheus," "Jericho," "Homage to Luigi Boccherini," "Musician at Court," "Meditation," "Sestina for Tea Time" appeared in SUITS FOR THE DEAD, published by Charles Scribner's Sons in 1961. "St. Patrick's Day: 47th Street," "Mouse," "Planting Crocus," "The Lemmings," "Elegy for Walter Stone," "Discussion, Back Home," "Family History," "Maquillage," "Mozart," "First Snow," "F. A. O. Schwarz," "Nursery Rime," "The School of Athens," "Belisarius," "A Victory for the Eastern Empire," "Colloquy Between Two Kings," "Variations on an Ancient Theme," "A Short Trot with Uccello's Horses," "Da Vinci Sunset," "Ride the High Country," and "Financial Statement" first appeared in THE CARNIVORE, published by the University of North Carolina Press in 1965. "Sestina for the Last Week of March," "Three Ideas of Disorder," "Precautions," "Pruning," "The Clearing," "Orleans Wreckers," "Fall," "Plymouth Rock," "Cape Cod House," "Exhortation to an Arab Friend," "Day Sailing," "A Compliment upon a Laugh," "Three Love Poems," "Uncles Wiggle Their Ears," "Lute," "The Covenant," "Tableau à la Rousseau," "Seals," "Epitaph for Goliath," "Dialogue in Ithaka," "Sapphic Fragments," "Jonah: A Report," "Prologue to a Play: Samuel Speaks," "Swoboda," "Leporello, in His Dressing Room," "The Death of Mozart," "Prolegomenon to the Study of Poetics," "Improvisation on Themes of John Donne," "Upon Receiving a Book of Poems," "Another Letter to Lord Byron" appeared in DAY SAILING, published by the University of North Carolina Press in 1969. "Surfers," "Dogs," "The Royal Canadian Air Force Exercises," "Monomoit Sharpening Stone," "Weeding: Florida, January," "Two Trees," "Black Grouper at Marathon," "Harbor," "Everglades: Bird Walk," "Telephones," "Love Song for Cello," "The Envoys," "Birthday Greetings—for Lynn," "The Voyeur," "Intellectual Women," "High Wire Act," "On a Lady from Philadelphia," "Soup," "Wishes," "Children's Story # 1," "Children's Story # 2," "Child's Play," "Children's Story # 3," "Riddle," "Jigsaw Puzzle," "Touring," "Three Adaptations from Catullus," "Peter de Luna," "St. Ebba of Coldingham," "Wordsworth's Music," "Art of Torture," "Sermonette," "Adaptations from the Swabian," "From the Notebooks of Da Vinci" appeared in CHILD'S PLAY, published by Louisiana State University Press in 1972.

For Lynn, as always

CONTENTS

NEW POEMS

I. VITAL SIGNS

II. AT HOME, IN THE WORLD

viii

III. TOUGH CHARACTERS

SELECTED POEMS

IV. IDEAS OF DISORDER

V. WOMEN AND CHILDREN

VITAL SIGNS
New and Selected Poems

NEW
POEMS

1
VITAL SIGNS

FOLLY

A dream machine, hot air in a bag;
crazy to try for Europe in it. Why?
It has never been done before. He wants to brag,
to be in the almanacs as much as the sky?

Such men are inarticulate, require
to float in our minds, gaudy dots in the thin
clouds of our rarest fancies, where the fire
of discontent will carry them. Who has not been

soiled by gravity's drag, the fate of weight
always to fall? The spirit soars, and the body
creeps among the necessities we hate,
accepts the inevitable, which is often shoddy.

There must have been something, somebody you wanted
and could not have, or something you wanted to be.
The hope died, but all of us are haunted
by the ghosts of an old dream, and it—or she—

can drive us crazy, reproaching, beckoning. Rage
turns hot, and the bag begins to swell,
and then, one morning, reading the front page,
we know he's crazy and still we wish him well.

Along with the food and water, a piece of each
of us is in that gondola, ballast, a grand
hope that folly, however absurd, might reach
impossible distances once and drift to land

safely in some glade where all our lost
loves will welcome us home with flowers, with kisses . . .

It's only an ocean. Of course it can be crossed.
Europe is large. There's Africa if he misses.

And yet, in a few days he disappears
first from the sky, then from the headlines, to drown
in the sea of disaster's news. We check our fears,
the ropes that hold us, keep us anchored down.

DRY BONES

A foot can lose its way. We come down wrong
on a sunny tennis court, or one dark night
trip where a root has heaved the pavement, and pain
shrills from the ankle. Ligaments that cling,
bind to inflexible bone the changeable meat,
give way. The doctors diagnose a sprain
but cannot heal the spirit's wound. We live,
passionate flesh hung on an orderly frame,
susceptible to tearing always, love
from honor, need from truth. In time
we may recover, but never again will walk
so carelessly. Small steps, and nervous eyes
scan the ground, fearful, and hurt, we talk
of how these dry bones, freed, one day may rise.

FOREIGN BODY

A foreign body will make the eyes tear,
will fester under the skin. We are xenophobes,
reject alien kidneys, hearts. Doctors
negotiate, their liberal black bags
full of blandishments, but the beast snarls
from inside its white cage a hatred of strangers.
We are separatists all, and our blood feuds
with other types. Children, innocent, die
from miscegenation of the factors. Bigots,
despots, each of us shrills from the balcony
me to the world's piazza. Still, there are truces,
treaties. Tourists learn *hello, goodbye,*
thank you, while dangerous men, polite, talk
careful nonsense at dinner tables and smile.
We are diplomats; we learn to be charming. The Czar
wants to acquire a warm-water port . . .
I have my secret instructions, as you have yours.
But then, one night, we forget who we are, ignore
what we are. I accept, crave, cling,
as if to a dream of peace, to your foreign body.

CONQUISTADOR

A paradise Peru! That the cities are gold
hardly matters. We leave the home country
for adventure, carrying beads, knives, mirrors,
to barter for empires. The French, English, Dutch,
the Portuguese and the Spanish worked it. Why not?

I gave you cheap trinkets, scraps of my life,
movies, meals, sometimes a bottle of wine,
and like a jungle queen you gave sapphires,
rubies, a vast treasure, but knew what I was.
You knew the ship moored in our cove would sail.
I am no prince except by your grace and patent.

Ashamed, I think of my holdings at home. A pauper
would stay with you; a grandee could afford to.
The ocean should have been real; the true distance
ought to have hidden us. We pretend the jungles,
lagoons, and simple savannahs in which we play.

I can't stand it. I can't not stand it.
I take shallow breaths, one at a time.

BEAST

A passion that hurts no one but me, a promise
of solace for rage, for hurt, on which no one relies,
a temporary order . . .
                            Why else write,
when the arms of women beckon, demand less,
and offer all—even the finest tears
that wait like grave rats for our eyes? I know,
being older than these lovelies, to love them
as a father would. Shakespeare settled for that
(or so we assume). But I am not he,
have not the imagination to let my servants
live my life, must do the work myself,
the dirty work.
                    I cut off the heads of chickens,
stick lobsters as old as my father in boiling water,
gut fish, and from time to time crush
girls like you. From appetite, from need.
Then sated from the mucking about, I write,
warn you and all your sisters, all my daughters,
the fish I catch, the game I pursue and love,
that beasts are on the loose, that I am one.

10

MAGIC

A rabbit from a hat, a playing card
from thin air, or scarves that come
out of an ear—it looks hard
to the uninitiated, but some
pros are out there watching, able
to judge the technique, do the trick
themselves, know where, under the table,
the rabbit is stashed. Their eyes are quick
as any hands, and their hearts as tough
as knowledge can make them. Peers, the star
plays to them, and they applaud
as loud as innocents seeing that stuff
for the first time—louder. We are
like them, know the tricks, are awed
that they still work: at first we desire
mystery, then learn to delight
in skill and style. I applaud your entire
repertoire more than on opening night.

BUS

As stops of organ pipes to a deaf man
must be theoretical, even theological, let us suppose
that the same theory, the same theology can
explain a crowd in a subway car or a bus,
can explain us. Who knows,

unable to hear the silent music playing?
We see the wind is up in that girl, or allowing a change
of instrument, of metaphor, that the graying
gentleman near the door who mutters and stammers
has been struck by hammers. The range

of orchestration is wide, and some of us sound
when the dampers are lifted, the harmonic overtones of our fellow
passengers. For no reason the heart will pound
in sympathy, want for their pains, their joys,
to make a noise, to bellow

unto the Lord, Who, presumably, can hear,
unless, like Beethoven, He too is deaf, deaf as a post,
and bangs at the keyboard . . . Oh, no, my dear,
struck, plucked, we must not think the notes
that died in our throats are lost.

FANFARE

1.

Behind the earnest woodwinds, glints of gold
promise what Midas dreamed: a stubbed toe
or the nerve of a tooth, but pleasure, a fire of joy.
He works the valves, joins his notes to the bold
crescendo that soon modulates to woe.
But then, for a moment, a flash, a twitch, a coy
suggestion of Tabasco wildness: riot!
orgy! execution! flesh that fries
in the mind's hot oil! The quivering quiet
of the strings is different as the echo dies
of that brief phrase, that immoderate riff. He sits
counting heartbeats, beating our time, and knows
more than we dare admit of those passionate fits
that threaten all our comfortable Jerichos.

2.

But tell the truth! Confess! It is my father;
Armando Ghitalla looks like my father, sits there
waiting, his head lowered, the jaw, the angle,
my father's when he's tired. Admit the idea
of my father playing the trumpet here, anywhere,
is crazy, though there ought to have been a life
of trumpet music, women, booze, fast cars,
high-stakes card games . . . My father had a cousin
who played the trumpet, was never mentioned, never
held up as model to strive for. Screw striving,
or let it balance out with pinky rings,
houndstooth jackets, coke spoons, the whole schmier,

because I don't know how to carry these things,
fear them, raise my voice sometimes in my room
when the amps are high and sing along with Brahms
(who used to play a fine whorehouse piano)
and weep for us both. The sons of criminals
are punished less! The trumpet, counselor?
It blows the mind right out through the bell,
and the juices flow out of the spit valve,
and it's brassy and vulgar, but still in any score
there is a place for trumpets, a need the ensemble
feels at its brightest moments for some wise-ass,
some precise freak to blast his heart out,
theirs, ours, and the music's. A gift, he couldn't
give it, nor dare it for himself. My father
playing the trumpet? It's almost as funny as me
playing the tuba mirum to wake the dead.

A PARTING

Correct, restrained, bereft,
we wished each other well.
You said, "You'd better go now," and I left.
It hurt like hell,

but flesh, disloyal, will heal,
and our hearts, fickle, mend.
Try as we may to hold it, the pain we feel
will come to an end.

Tenderness turns to tough
scar tissue. We lose the nerve,
can suffer no more than we loved. It's never enough,
but it's what we deserve.

L'ELISIR D'AMORE

Demented Italians on stage bellow and wail
of love, of love gone bad, of fate, its pain . . .
They are never loud enough. We are not convinced;
our lives are not like that. And then, one day,
one week, we fall apart. Decorum fails
and conversation falters, and in our hearts
we hear the arias echo, true after all,
and still not loud enough to fill the silence
or mask the kettledrums in the pits of our ears.
You meet someone, you leave someone, you quarrel
and think of leaving, or some nights you are happy:
at such times you must be a tenor, sing,
and let her be a soprano. We have hit
impossible notes together. Silent again,
we resume our series seats and hear the performers
do just what we have done, singing our scores.
Here and there in the house, *una furtiva
lagrima* gleams, talent without the voice,
one of the villagers' chorus, one of us.

RELAXATION

Easier than I thought: an attitude,
a few modest gestures arranged on the page
correctly, and I am there, having made my mark.
Mastery, discipline, difficulty bore me.
I've done that, and want to relax, to be
another happy fool writing lines that do not
come out to the right side of Bentham's page.
All those years, I sat up in my chair,
feet on the floor, back straight, eyes right
on the paper . . .
           And what was the good?
                If you love me,
it is not because I am learned, clever, adept,
nor for my proper posture. If you love me,
it is something mysterious, something I never noticed
that appeals to you—perhaps in the way I sprawl.
All those strenuous performances?
Worthless, all of them worthless, or nearly. You liked
the way I looked after I had finished,
the way I grinned, wiped the sweat from my eyes,
and flopped down on the floor like a tired child.

FALLING

Falling is faster than drowning. The life, its mistakes
do not flash back in painful review mixed
with redundant ocean salt. There is a mess
at the end, of course, but during the fall less
struggle, a feeling of freedom from the fixed
laws—except for gravity's. One takes
the positions of swimming, of dancing. That fluid grace
is better late than not at all. A cliff,
a tall building, a bridge, and all that space
can make the knees go watery, the stiff
neck sag, as once or twice ardor
did, and I leapt and survived. Do I make a third
and final effort, only a little harder,
to end this beastliness and be a bird?

"BREAK, BREAK, BREAK"

Five in the morning, a tough time . . . The light
of a false dawn that drains you chews at the rocks
as if they were fruit. You walk, and the earth's crust
seems dangerously thin, the ice of a night
across a pond. All composure cracks.
Beneath is all roiling and shifting. Thus, you must
imagine Tennyson grieving, scared. The old
manner has changed but the pain hasn't. Read
the poet into the stones, awash, cold,
eroding. With what style should a man bleed?
Rocks give way. The tallest crag hung
out over the water precariously
will crumble any time—a young tongue
in an old ear will make the sound of the sea.

CINDERELLA

Forget the sister, stepmother; the point
is the change from coach to pumpkin, of horses and footmen
to rats, frogs, whatever . . . that Cinderella,
queen of the night, turns commoner again,
not at midnight (for children one has to shuffle
mysteries, trade one wild card for another)
but whenever she and the prince have had their time,
and they fall asleep, away, as the night's magic
collapses. The dawn is not deceived. We stagger
through a natural light as cruel as nature is,
blink, rub our eyes. The flannel bathrobe
you put on in the morning is less than nothing:
naked you wore lust's cloth of gold, love's
seed pearls, the diadem of wonder,
and all of the night's gaudy regalia. You offer
coffee: "Sugar? Cream?" The black questions
of strangers rumble past like the noises of traffic.

Well, Cinderella, what is there to say?
Let us be polite to each other, get through
the damned day, and maybe we'll be lucky
as in the story. What the magic wand has done
it can do again. There are sometimes second chances.
Some princes come back, and some dreams
reflect us better, truer than bathroom mirrors.
We are nervous, tender with one another, tender
ourselves, and, shy, we hope that the shoe fits.

LOVE SONG ON A COLD PRAIRIE

Greedy for futures once, I staked my claims,
hacked prospects, hewed a present, learned to hold . . .
I hold you now, but lightly, whittling moments
with which to furnish a past. We cling together
and over each other's shoulders see different horizons.
What you have yet to learn, I am unlearning.
Our eyes scan the terrain, the rumpled bedclothes
where we pitched camp. You will not settle here,
nor can I blame you, looking to dig my grave.
It's clear; it's cold; these embers of our fire
will last us through to dawn when we'll move on.

MENDING NETS

Holes tied together? But make them mouths,
webs of hunger to seize in their tightening skeins
fish for the village where we see them hanging
to dry in a wash of late afternoon sunlight
as crude as the local pastis. Fancies bud
in this agreeable air, and, sheltered, blossom
upon our boredom, gaudy bromeliads.
We sit in a garden, drink, look out at the sea,
and, like that last boat out past the point,
that animated dot, the mind trawls.

An effort just to sit and imagine effort:
the casting out, the hope, the hauling in
from depths those monstrous riches that writhe, roiling
black water silver . . . The living truth?
or have we snagged on a rock, a crop of coral,
with a tearing as silent as good minds giving way?

Even to watch the mending of nets is mending.

SCI-FI SEQUENCE

1.

I have learned this hill,
know where edible plants grow,
where rabbits hide, where springs flow,
have eaten—if not my fill,

at least enough to live—
should be grateful. It does no good
to rage that the place that long fed
me has no more to give.

2.

Leave. It's as simple as that, but others have gone
down to the plain where savage beasts or men
have stripped them to white bones, or higher, to mountains
where I have ventured only in summers and found them
frozen. It's bad. One does not know the water.
Finding a cave, a sheltering log, takes days.
Every sound is strange and therefore a danger.
Fear fights with fatigue, and both with hunger.
The odds are awful, and yet there is hope—a pass
somewhere through those mountains, another valley,
a richer hill than this, where, if I'm lucky,
they will not kill me. It depends on the women there,
consulting their needs, tastes, whims, asking,
after I've borne so much, am I still pleasing.

3.

Cunning and health—if I can carry
these, I carry more than I need.
And maybe a little pride? I'm sorry

to leave these fires, but shall not plead
with women who turn their backs to me.
They have themselves, their children to feed,

and do what they must. And I must flee
though not appearing to do so. Or stay
at the edge of the camp, and let them see

me starve slowly until one day
they find my body and don't react.
Better to take my chances away

from here, from them. As a matter of fact,
pride weighs more than love, fear,
or even hunger. I exact

more from life than any mere
women can. I shall disappear,
and if I die, it won't be here.

4.

Believe that shit? You don't
believe that shit. I don't
want to leave, don't want
to die, to risk dying, run
like an animal from animals, grub
after grubs. That kind of living
is not living. Why should they make

me want to, why should they want to
make me leave? I am no worse
than other men, no worse than they,
know this hill, this place, this
life. They are not my fault,
bad times, scarce food. Hungry,
I regret that children are hungry,
and girls, old women . . . No, curse
girls, old women, all women
who do this to anyone, or not
to anyone, but to me, and swear
vengeance, there will be vengeance: men
will exact a worse price and make
women pay for this, seize their
power, use them as badly, worse,
cast them out from the warmth of fires,
them and their children with them. Men
who live in swamps, mad or not
mad but sane and wronged—the eyes
glare either way—when they capture women . . .
I cannot imagine what they do,
never tried. The swamp fevers
are fevers of imagination;
their eyes may shine bright from dreams,
the possibility that justice
is the fair sharing of suffering,
or that men may light their own fires,
turn to each other, sing and dance
in joy when a son is born, and bear
ourselves the joy that should have been

our own, our fathers'. Not on this hill,
and not in this lifetime . . . Reason enough
to light out, take off? I must try
to believe; I must believe, must try.

5.
Something like that happened, must
have happened. We can feel it still
who sometimes see a brother bust
out, take off into the chill
thickets, sick of himself, of this
slow death at the edge of the light
the fires spread like honey. His
tracks disappear, but then, at night,
howls, cries, strange kinds of noise,
neither from animal nor bird,
filter back. It's one of the boys.
None of us mentions what we've heard,
but again it echoes one afternoon
in the men's hut when the palm wine
is flowing and some poet-buffoon
works that howl into a line
of the tame epic we've heard before.
A cough, a giggle, as at an obscene
joke, and we glance through the open door
to the jungle, inviting, thick, and green.

TRAUMA

I remember the sound of the door's slam
on my finger, the look of the blood's drip
on one white shoe, but somehow I am
excused from recalling the pain. The tip

of the finger looks fine now, except
for that second moon in the fingernail
which over the course of months has crept
out from the first, the track of a snail

or a slug trail in my body's garden.
Hidden in the insulted cells,
the memory remained to harden
into the growing nail. Time tells,

but takes its time as it cultivates
the sins of childhood, of fathers. Warmed
by a generous sun, we grow. It waits,
and then, one day, we are deformed.

A NOTE TO THE PSALMIST

If my right hand lose its cunning,
will I forget thee, O Jerusalem?
I have been set in a high place.
Why have I been cast down?
The faithful rejoice;
or do those who rejoice have the faith?
How can adversity teach, or loss instruct?
My pain disfigures me.
From joy to competence, I was thrust out.
I can barely remember the kingdom of my childhood.
From competence, where shall I go?
To the cold tundra? to fields of ice?
My fingers are numb. The pen feels strange in my hand.
My life runs dry.
O Lord, relent, let the fingers feel,
give me back my life, and let me climb
green hills again, where olives grow,
or let me forget such hills, such gleaming cities.
Have mercy. Let me forget Jerusalem.

NIGHT CREATURES

Imagine imagination that varies inversely
with being, so that elephants must lack it,
barely able to grasp their own bulk and weight
as they must be also deficient in deviousness,
thinking in straight lines from which they scarcely
waver, hacking trails of vectors with racket
they hardly notice, bulling toward a mate . . .
We must be cleverer, think more, being less,
who, to scamper from cover, must risk our lives,
touch only briefly, but dream and remember long,
like mice, like voles, those brave fools of the night
all men with mistresses become, whose wives
trumpet the truth: that we are small and wrong
and hopeless, and they are angry, huge, and right.

REMORSE

"All I learned is what I love."
　　　　　　　　　　　　　　—Roethke

Is there any other study but desire?
The leaves learn the sun; the plants turn
giddy with wisdom. We are slower, shyer,
and rust with caution where we ought to burn,
love ourselves too little, others less,
and go to our graves stupid. O Lord, bless
the whims that should have been passions. Forgive our fears.
We had great chances, and lost them with our small
souls which crust with remorse for all those years
of riotous dreams, having slept through them all.

30

THE BIG SPENDERS

Keen for our baubles, our attic junk,
the proud droves arrive, whimsically rich,
the big spenders, the young. We make a dollar
who once, ourselves, as lavishly as they
and passionate to own, invested, plunged.
It's no good. Money runs out, and time.
We are all impoverished sooner or later, and learn,
by harder lessons than these punks can imagine,
our limitations. Which of us still tries
to acquire Italian, to master the calculus,
to possess all the symphonies of Haydn?
Oh, we still go to the Square, will window-shop,
pop for a cheap but amusing trinket, or bargain
for something more expensive we don't need
except to complete some useless, lavish collection.
We have no credit, can no longer buy on time,
have lost our student-discount cards, are enrolled
in another program now—in which we study
the art of admiring and of letting go.

RECITATION

Like one of those stupid boys who choose a seat
three-quarters back in the class in which to hide,
we are startled, look around, rise to our feet
slowly when joy calls on us. Inside
we know the answer, but which of us can show
the grace, the lightness? We make a gorilla grin,
dance like a circus bear with a stubbed toe,
whimper a tuneless song, as if we were in
great pain. There are even tears on our faces
we smear at with clumsy fists. The moment fades;
there is laughter in the room when we sit down.
They do not know what the teacher knows. The spaces
in the little book on her desk where she enters grades
fill up with a row of 'A's for the class clown.

THE TRUST

Like wax, my father's tears burned on my skin
and froze like lead into these hard places,
tough to the world; yet, like a child I pick,
pick, hoping to heal, to feel again.

There should be some myth for it, some bizarre
monster, the pain of whose wounds was shared—foe,
stranger, and friend suffering too. The Greeks . . .
were less imaginative? kinder than we are?

who hurt, expect to hurt, each, unless
virtue continue for seven generations
to excuse some child somewhere. Two billion souls:
how few must be the heirs of sinlessness!

Which of us would breed, bearing the mark
of a grandfather's hurt in trust for a great-grandson?
A girl on a rug; a room on a dry day;
and like Michelangelo's drowsy Adam, we spark.

Pull back? Ignore it? Fight the monster? Bid
it back to its maculate lair? Sometimes we do.
Pretending to be normal, I offer a drink,
dinner, the rest . . . as my father did.

HIJACKERS

Metal detectors, X-ray machines, the three
uniformed guards, armed, standing close to the gate
protect us from ourselves. For security
we allow their prying, empty our pockets, wait

as they paw through our carry-on baggage, sift through our lives'
trinkets and secrets. Our dirty underwear
bores them; they are looking for guns and knives
or bombs hidden in unlikely places. They stare,

hostile, suspicious as we pass through; they are lazy,
and miss the telephone numbers we have jotted
on our ticket envelopes. No Arab crazy
or Cuban desperado could have plotted

an enterprise more unlikely: "Take this plane
to Algiers, Katmandu, the Pribilofs. Fly
from airport to airport, escalating insane
demands—a million dollars and parachutes." Try

anything! Take risks! The passengers pray,
hostages for our ride, but what can they lose?
Their scheduled lives' connections at JFK?
How did it happen? Gelignite in our shoes?

Simpler than that—all the secrets, the guilt,
the grief in those briefcases, in critical mass,
can explode at any time. The planes are not built
to take such stress. The laughter in first class

is far too brittle. The tourist section's a shambles.
The stewardesses are weeping. The captain gives in.

The plane will do what we want. The airline gambles
that sooner or later security people will win.

But in the meantime, love, we bargain for time.
Do we go together to Pago Pago to play
in a hijackers' heaven worth any capital crime,
or die not even trying, the coward's way?

CONFESSION

"A book—there a man gives birth to what a woman begat."

—Karl Kraus

My years of training in arrogant technique,
certain as treasury bills, their yield small
but sure, my life in good order . . . all gone.
I am a girl picked up by a dazzling rogue
whose boots track mud through the chambers of my heart.
I hate him, hate myself, want to go back,
but melt, my knees melt.
                    All those years
are with me still, amuse him. He likes my diction
as I echo the truths I learn from his sensuous lips.

THE WRITING ON THE WALL

Naked, as I imagine you always, but younger,
you started out omnipotent—your yell
brought somebody to deal with thirst and hunger.
It couldn't last; you spoke and broke the spell.
You learned what all of us learn, that powers shrink
to what we can do for ourselves. We are all deposed
to the age of reason where you live now. You think
you've suffered loss enough? Once I supposed
the same thing, until I saw the wall
the anarchists had painted their signs on: "Death
to . . ." Me? Immortal, beautiful, we fall.
I did. You shall. It takes away the breath.
As once your father smoothed your unfurrowed brow
with comfort in advance, I hold you now.

GLARE

Old men and women appear to bask in the sun,
seem to delight in the pleasures of fresh air,
the caress of warmth on wattles, wrinkles, spots,
the flash of the lids' redness through blear eyes
to the tired retinas . . . Or that's what we think
who are younger, have not learned their mean tricks,
do not know that rage or grief or pain
will contort the features, turn a plausible face
into a grimace as ugly as its cause,
or that on those benches one can let the sun
take the blame away, its glare an excuse:
a squint can look like grief, resemble rage,
pass for human, and counterfeit a peace
that dark and cold will soon enough turn real.

CALENDARS

Old years curl on the wall, their offerings
flyblown now—girl's flesh, mountains, a flower.
Who still believes their promises? Who clings
to the dreams of love, achievement, or peace that our
plumber, our banker will mail for us to nail
on the same wall, new hopes for our old debris?
We have learned that only failure cannot fail.
Mountains? Flowers? With weaker, wiser eyes,
we watch as the dust collects a certainty
we must have felt once, girdled in those thighs.

SPONTANEOUS GENERATION

Spallanzani, the theory holds
as well as ever: generation
is, I say, spontaneous. Garbage breeds
maggots; bread makes mold;
a box with wood shavings left in the dark
long enough will make mice.
                                    No? Never?
But look at those cultural centers built to breed
a vigorous theater, music . . .
                                    So cargo-cults
on out-of-the-way Pacific islands dance,
light torches and wait for ships, supply planes to come
as they did in World War II.
                                    I clean my desk,
fill my pen, and place a fresh yellow pad
centered on the blotter, waiting for poems.

A LAMENT, FOR MY WIFE

Speech betrays. We have talked to one another,
promising, endlessly qualifying, refining . . .
What's unsaid is still true, that I shall desert you
sooner or later, and not just a late night
nor weekend away—no such kind subterfuge—
but openly leave, for a cold, silent woman
with whom I am speechless, to whom I shall be faithful
as I have never been. What is there to say?
That I should stay with you, comfort, protect?
That I am behaving badly? My dear, I know,
but I have seen her in concert halls, in shops
where we have exchanged glances. I looked away,
but it was settled. I know that she will have me,
will take me into her irresistible arms.

COCKROACHES

Sugar, even glue . . . They will eat
anything. They scurry from light
but return when the dark falls, discreet,
to girls' apartments, a common sight.
We recognize ourselves, confrères,
for like the roaches I invade
these railroad flats, have climbed dark stairs
in hunger for sweetness, for glue, have stayed
through the same looks of disgust and reproach
and fled the slipper and poison can.
Franz Kafka's enormous roach
was not so special: every man
puts on that shiny carapace,
twiddles his feelers once in a while,
thinks of flight from his ordered place
and longs for a litter of laundry, a style
of chipped coffee mugs and laughter
in spite of the flat, in spite of all
the bugs—whom I shall see hereafter
and greet in another ill-lit hall.

THE BEDS OF STRANGERS

That flesh be rendered to tallow, rough made smooth,
and knobby differences be resolved, we wallow
in the beds of strangers, hoping for that flash
that will make the wick burst into flame. The dark
threatens us, as the light indicts—and we yearn
for a flattering glow that will turn these strange rooms
familiar, make them our own, and let the mirrors
show us a new face with the lines gone,
the eyes burning like candles with youth and strength.
The vision dazzles old hopes back to life:
we dream of dreaming ourselves together and melting.
But it never happens, or never enough. We try
and later remember the sparks, the hints and glimpses,
as we struck, one on another, our flinty hearts.

CLINGING

The flowers were crude, charming but too direct,
their voluptuous petals, sepals, stamens, pistils
making such easy suggestions of summer affairs
which do not last. In the late fall we inspect
our bare woods, tramp our austere hills
and learn from the tangling vines a love that wears
through seasons of cold. They twine, writhe, cling
in erotic riot, but slow, in a long embrace
no blossom can match. Let giants bring
forests in with your coffee: on your face
let my fingers take root like that. Mistletoe,
wisteria, rambler roses . . . The tendril fingers
hold on after the summer flowers go
in a passion the more impressive the more it lingers.

CRUISING

The weather changes, wind shifts,
tide turns, and too far
from the fixed line in all this heaving
blue-gray, I pitch into panic,
roll in regret for my carelessness. How
was I seduced by the glint of light
dancing on water, the pillow puffs
of cloud in the sky? Ride it out!
Bail, scramble, pray, promise
never to venture so far again,
never to sail again, to sell
the damned boat . . .
                 Later, alive,
land-legs back, and feeling better,
I am proud of myself for having survived,
and warmed with rum forget the prayers,
the extravagant promises. Try again,
when blue shall beckon and billow call
of sky and sea, or eye and bosom,
in bed or boat to reach and haul
from tricky winds pleasure and more?
Boats are made to sail in; men
are given to choose—to go down in them
or on the beach to die of dry rot.
The lines of a vessel can dance at rest,
tease to be tried, to move. Come,
haul anchor, love, haul ass.

PRODIGY

Their smallness matters more than their sex. Depraved,
bored by the scores we have heard before, we attend
to their frilly dresses, their short pants, and the grave
way they walk out with a maestro who isn't their friend
to take their places on raised-up piano benches
and perform what they've been taught—one movement, the next,
amusing us old roués. Grown lads and wenches
could do it better, adults of whom one expects
proficiency, passion. An Arab brothel child,
a prodigy, a protégé, appears
a like creature of our desires, remote
from what he does, and therefore charming. The wild
innocence is the same that perseveres
through all the perverse cadenzas he's learned by rote.
It's our last hope. Splotched childishness, we pray
by all the passions we've wallowed in for years,
will save us, or drag him down—for either way
we shall be equals again. The applause he hears
is music to his ears, and his eyes shine,
exposed, infected with the first touch of the queer
malaise we recognize. The concert was fine;
we shall follow with some interest his career.

THE PIRATE

Tidied as my nursery was, my childhood,
all its mess stored in that wooden trunk
with its benign pirate sharing my secrets,
will pass inspection: guests, my friends, play,
miss the cowboy doll under the bed
where I cried for hours, and nobody can see
the imaginary friend who understood
everything, was never bored, who liked me
better than I have learned to like myself.
"Turn back . . ." I have written the phrase and stopped
a dozen times. To find what? Pain?
I have that now, and study, like an arthritic,
its pirate face, look in the unpatched eye
for company, for comfort, vital signs.

STAG NIGHT

Torn to shreds in the beds of women, men
would turn to one another, would speak, cannot.
I tell you, sirs, we are better than they say,
braver than we know ourselves, and gentle.
What do we want for our pain but moments of comfort?
For this they rack us. No, do not feel grief.
Turn it outward, lest it infect the guts.
Rage will ruin digestion. Better survive.
The only sane emotion may be anger.
We must love ourselves, pick up from the floor
what dignity we can, and with reserve,
with great restraint, and our shoes in our hands, walk
slowly away, like little boys, jaws clenched,
and eyes as dry as if it had not hurt.

GIFTS

We do not choose our gifts; they come, surprises,
at awkward moments, long before we are ready,
or late, after our souls are stiff with longing,
curious presents we could not have dared imagine
from those we love, from strangers, from out of the sky . . .
They embarrass us with their opulence, weigh us down,
turn us away from our reasonable pursuits.

As parents we know the difficulty, to balance
too much, too little, too early, too late, to contrive
the steady flow of toys, of clothing, of love
that will not enrage, distract, spoil, ruin
the child as we have been ruined by dazzling gifts,
or embittered. Oh, the dawns I have slept through,
the golden mornings I have wasted, drinking
Alka-Seltzer after wasted nights.
Beauties, riches, love, and none of it fit
my rigid intentions, my laziness, my life.

Yet we would not be churls. We have good manners,
give thanks and praise for all the treasures given,
no matter how cruel their indictments. Squanderers, fools,
we say the decent things and then, in our rooms,
weep for the splendid selves our gifts deserved.

PRAYER FOR A DAUGHTER

We want to live forever in our own persons,
but, willing to settle for surrogates, we pray
that God will give us sons, grandsons, a line
of male selves, somehow our own flesh.
And we get daughters, and we are shocked like Shahs,
but learn to love like fathers, and learn to die.
They grow on us. We try to ignore the truth—
they are beauty and youth and life and not for us.
The best of us protect them and let them go.
More civil than the cavaliers were with headsmen,
we make a jest, a compliment, are gallant
as men can be in pain. My living heart
will throb in her fist; my chest will be torn hollow.
I pray for a last breath to say "God bless."

CENTRAL CASTING

Bogart: It was my health. I came to Casablanca for the waters.
Raines: Waters? What waters? We're in the desert!
Bogart: I was misinformed.

—*Casablanca*

When infirmity, disease seize us, prod,
delve for mischief, chief among their prizes
are mental: ambition, will will wilt like wax
in the heat of fever, fall fallow with the break,
and then from our exhaustion grow grotesque new selves
we try to recognize. Eyes peering back from a gaunt mirror
search for a vanity we'd have thought ought to have survived.

We convalesce, yes, and mend
as the multiplying cells salvage a kind of self
no longer perfect, factory fresh, a slight second.
For the other, the inner, the image, major adjustments:
vanity dawdles so, and pride rides a high but slow horse.
Having so scampered away, startled, the star of our secret
bio-pic, our super Cooper or even our puny Muni,
may never return, and we turn to the character actors
we must settle upon and sign, resigned to being that.

GRACE BEFORE MEALS

When the fodder has given out, the farmer slaughters.
Famine often begins with a terrible feast.
It's difficult for the innocent sons and daughters,
or the wife who has seen it before like this, increased
and then gone. How to let them feel
the giddy joy of the present? We learn to sup
like the mad, the old, who know that any meal
could be their last, and gaily gobble up.

SUCCESSION

Whig sons and Tory fathers—of course!
We read of the old wars, remembering ours:
the tyrant smelled of lavender after-shave,
kissed us goodnight, and rode off on his horse
to exercise, for us, those awesome powers
we had to challenge and subvert. "God save
the king!" we shouted, but still we made him sign
the vote, the privy purse to us. The line
is longer than the Bourbons'. We are each
pretenders, exiles, rebels. We succeed
to find the throne is weaker than we had guessed,
and to learn what we had once presumed to teach
of power and love, as new crown princes read
about old tyrants, and lump us with the rest.

EXILE

With a studied stride and a countenance neither proud
nor cringing, which is not easy with jewels in your boots—
what's left of the family fortune you've smuggled out—
you stare down the customs inspectors, stare down at the schmutz
of your old life, caked and clinging still.
You hand them the forms. There's nothing to declare;
it's hardly news that old regimes can fall.
Where will you settle, and what will you settle for?
They're questions you wonder about, as in a novel
you don't much like but feel compelled to get through.
The gems make it hard to walk, but the real pain
is in the shabbiness. Cuffs, lives unravel,
and you are proud of it still. Live, and buy new!
The mud that falls away will collect again.

STORMS

You can see the storms on maps, their plotted isobars
    wild as a mountain range, an ocean floor,
wilder, moving, the chasms now yawning in Kansas
    on their way here, and leaves will give way, fall
revealing the structures of tree trunks forking to branches, branches
    spreading to twigs, in a clarity the young
admire, their foolish hot heads longing to be cool.
Older, we know that sticks are sticks, that lines
were there all the time, known, remembered from other winters,
    and cold, ourselves, we think of the summers' riot,
the burgeoning of hope, the thriving of lust's green health
    they take for granted, assume as a right, vacations
from the business of living, a chance to scurry away to play
    by the seashore or into the mountains until
one year the mountains come, as they would not to Mohammed,
    and a Moho opens up beneath the feet,
while Lear's storm rages, and hopes, leaves, leave us
    old, clear, grieving, afraid the sun
may not come back, there may be no more limitless Mays,
    no more July fullness, October flare.
The lines of our biographies come clear, shorn
    of that undervalued green that was what we were.

II

AT HOME,
IN THE WORLD

SETTLING IN

1.

They join at last or separate; the flesh
releases or receives the troubled spirit.
Moonlight silvers the water—rising or setting—
till all that silver comes to rest in darkness.
We peer ahead and take our best sights
from what we have learned of sex or what we remember
of infancy. Or look to the nearly mad,
marathon runner, violinist, or driver
of racing cars, who disappoint us, mumbling
nonsense into the microphones. From wild
frontiers they bring us banal rocks. It's subtle,
commonplace; it's what we all know
who dwell in our body's other (sickness and age
have nothing to do with *us*) and are dispossessed
first of that robust, agile, keen corpus,
and then, more cruel, of hope: The rentier
is not the pal we leaseholders believed.

2.

The houses we have lived in, plucked and trucked
on wide-load flatbeds over the interstate,
arranged along a single block would make
a street to bear our name, fit for us.
Remember a Rothschild azalea in gaudy bloom
houses ago? As easily remember
my index finger before the curved scar.
With aching feet we walk down that dream street.

3.

To furnish a house is to furnish lives—to flesh
ideas as deep as that sea grotto, dank
with the salt of dream-sweat more than the sea,
to salvage, dripping brine and ooze, the hulks
of our sunken souls. More, we propitiate
the household gods, Lares Familiares,
who pour our precious time from horn to cup.
Any house is a temple: The shutters, the floors,
the hidden places that rattle or creak or sigh,
inspirited by winds, proclaim it so,
returning a tithe on lives we have invested.
Why else drive a kilometer out of the way
to see where Flaubert lived, or look with wonder
at Dickens' inkwell still stained that bright blue?

Habitat, lair, spoor—we make our tracks
that glisten like the trails of garden slugs.

4.

The first of the practical arts has got to be breathing,
that fragile exchange with the world; the rest follows—
taking in the tang of where we are
and then exhaling, to mark for a moment the cold
pane with cartoon ghosts.
                              In certain rooms
one inhales in delight or admiration;
in others, one breathes out, sighing. We paint,
drape, carpet, invest . . .
                              Like hermit crabs
that search for the right shell, large enough

for comfort and yet small enough to carry,
we too forage for husks among the dead
and settle in.
          And learn? And take on what?

That rug. Two men in Persia worked for years
making that, both of them long dead.
Knotted into the pile are crooked footprints
of the old Boston City Hall gang. The red
is from crushed bodies of insects they used for dye,
but all of it is dye, the sweat and the money
as surely as the bugs. My children walk it,
innocent as astronauts. Their bikes
down in the garage gleam cheerful chrome
where owners of this place once sought the darkness.
Killed themselves, I mean. The last image
upon their retinas? A shelf at the back
for storing garden tools, and the shape of a trowel.
Meaning? Perhaps nothing, or almost nothing.
Maybe: We should go lightly where we light.

5.

Lares and Manes, genii loci,
wisps that float on the dawn, shimmer off
in the glare of the workday and its conceits,
but return like cats to bestow their presences
which we can neither avoid nor try to deserve.

Across the street, a graveyard: "America's oldest
Garden Cemetery . . . immortal beauty . . .
praised by poets and horticulturists . . .

since its consecration in 1831."
No bicycling. No rubbings. From our doorstep,
I can see PICKERING, Edward C.
(Am. Astronomer) near the corner
of Maple Avenue and Acorn Path.
Down toward Mount Auburn, by Halcyon Lake, Mary
Baker Eddy (Am. nut) does not
have a visible phone line hooked up to her tomb,
unless they've buried that, too.
                           But Lowell, James R.
(and Amy). And Holmes. Longfellow. What Cambridge,
what America was, they were.
                       "Any verse
that makes you and me foreigners," said Lowell,
"is not only not great poetry but no
poetry at all."
                Class of '35,
Harvard. Studied with Longfellow. Ambassador
to Spain. Ambassador to the Court of St. James.
Old, he returned to Cambridge, gave the Lowell
lectures again, in '87, and died
in '91 at Elmwood, the family place.
Him, a foreigner?
               Ask, better, Slavotsky,
the tailor, then ready to schlepp, via Paris, London,
and New York, to Bridgeport: *Any life*
that makes you and me foreigners is (etc.)
. . . *no life at all.*
               But we have settled.

Native now, my namesake grandfather
is rooted in the soil as deep as Lowell
who said that poetry should be too, "not
in the grovelling fashion of the potato" but
"aspiring" like "the pine that climbs forever
toward diviner air."

                  I like potatoes
Eyes that come to life, sprout rootlets, force
through rocky ground, aspire, first, to life.
The breaking through to air, light, blossom,
comes in its good time. And we have come,
cautious as the beavers of the Charles
that venture to the higher ground for the bark
of trees that grow near Mary Eddy's pond—
which is, by rights, theirs who lived here first,
even before the Lowells. We came later,
and must propitiate those dignified
unfashionable spirits, placate, assure:
They are not, will not be foreigners here.

6.

It's easier with Oliver Wendell Holmes,
which speaks less well for either of us than for this
disprized land we have come to share.

                             Remember
the scene: Dr. Livingstone, I presume?
Mr. Stanley . . .

               But sillier:

                     Stanley?

                          Oliver!

Hardy? Or Dr. Holmes?
                              To whom I'd be glad
to play Mr. Watson. Out of this jumble
in which he and I are both foreigners,
there are yet discernible strands of pattern
as in a frayed rug. Both our fathers,
after all, were Yale men.
                              Both of us
studied in the hall that Bulfinch built
at Andover.
                    (Charlie's here. On Bellwort Path.)
The lines are clear as Holmes' descent from Bradstreet:
        Still, as the spiral grew,
He left the past year's dwelling for the new,
Stole with soft step its shining archway through,
        Built up its idle door,
Stretched in his last-found home . . .

"The Chambered Nautilus." Better than we remember.
The book I copy goes back twenty years
to that green time I spent at school on the hill,
where, in the library named for him, I studied,
punched an exotic time-clock.
                              Leisure, grace
are matters of luck, mostly. "Build thee more stately
mansions"?
                O my soul! The silver platter
runneth over, for all of us here on Brattle,
on Coolidge Hill. We are the foreigners, where
ἄξιον is a brand of detergent, and nothing
worthy is left but what we pretend to remember.

64

7.

Walking the dog, learning the hill at night,
I have often seen the cars. Lovers park
up past the last house, where the dead forbear
or are, at least, discreet. And if I mind,
it isn't them but the thought of their discomfort,
the awkwardness, the cold, that I'm getting older,
am settling in, am further down that block
than I had thought. Next to the last house?
Across the street are the last houses, for poets
and horticulturists too. There's a fence around it
to keep the vandals out. But they are in.
Only the young are natives here, the brash,
the energetic, vulgar, healthy children
that once we were, and then supposed we were.
The dog sniffs, pees. I take him inside,
turn out the lights, lock up. Later I hear
the motors of those cars, in need of mufflers,
roaring through our civil dreams like beasts.

A DISQUISITION ON CATS

The keeping of cats is a serious matter,
for all manner of men have considered them, what they are in grace,
        in play, in repose, and what they mean,
and tried to entertain, as the cat entertains, or to make the cat
        carry, as mad Smart tried with his Jeoffry,
the burden of our lives, to provide with those wise eyes, those elegant
        whiskers, answers.
But if we are hasty, if we are inattentive, the prey will surely
        escape,
for we must learn to study with the cat's patience, to sit
        at the mousehole, to keep still.

His courtliness makes every house a court and each of us a king,
for there have been greats and terribles, and mostly indifferent
        kings,
but all of them, all of us, mighty. And cats serve might,
but will not fawn, will show us by their manners what we should be
        to deserve such manners.
The daintiness at the supper dish, the silent tread, the fastidious
        grooming, the attentive eyes
oblige us to improvement. And we fail. And they say nothing,
        show nothing, and oblige us further.
The rustic barons out in the fields, our pals, the dogs, make no
        demands,
but a cat is minister of finance, is ambassador from a nearly always
        friendly country, is the herald-at-arms
upon whom we know the kingdom depends, which is why we sit
        a quarter of an hour without moving, lest we disturb
        the cat on our lap in a sleep that may be feigned.

At the feet of Pollio's statue of Libertas in Tiberius Gracchus's
      temple,
below the cap of independence and the rod magistrates used for
      the manumission of slaves,
there was a cat curled up, watchful, for no cat will endure
      constraint—
which makes it right that Napoleon had a morbid fear of cats.
Yet will they accommodate themselves, will suit, as their convenience
      suits them, will repay intelligent attention
with intricate and oblique assurance of trust:
as, for example, sleeping in the presence, for sleeping in the
      presence of power is faith in us;
or clowning with a ball of wool, as courtiers will, to amuse.
To be precise, the saying should be revised: Only a cat
      knows how to look at a king.
That long, narrowed gaze, the slow blink, the imperturbability . . .
Richelieu always carried a kitten. When it grew, he replaced it
      with another,
wishing, I should think, not to be outdone, not to be surpassed
      by a grown cat more subtle, more adept than any cardinal.

See how he crouches, how he leaps and lands, or notice the claws
      that splay from between the pads, and examine the tearing
      teeth
all which proclaim the family, Felidae—lions, tigers,
      panthers, jaguars, cougars, pumas, cheetahs, lynxes . . .
What man first tamed the wildcat's kitten, took him in, to endure
      the slashes, the scratches,
for an intimacy with excellence, for pride?
The rest of the village must have been amazed, must have acknowledged
      the keeper of the cat as magician, priest, or chief . . .

Or Lord Mayor? But old Dick Whittington's cat was a coal boat,
        deep-waisted, narrow-sterned, trading from Newcastle.
The children's story turns the cat-boat into *Le Chat Botté*,
          the amazing Puss in Boots who got for his master,
             Constantine,
          a castle, a princess, a fortune in Straparola's tale.
They like wealth, but, true aristocrats, they never need it,
          can live hard and yet retain that air, that silken, sinewy
          bon ton of which they are the masters.
Master that, and the rest of the world is yours.

Diodorus tells us that in Egypt, where cats were gods, the killing
          of a cat, even by accident, was punished by death:
a hard rule, but in responsibilities begin our best dreams,
          and the keeping of cats, as I say, is a serious business,
a relationship of delicacy, of tact, of extension, of forbearance,
          which is to say of love.
Because it is easy to love ourselves, or those who are close to us,
          but to cherish difference is a mark of stature and our
          only hope of heaven—
literally, for what could God need with men, what use could He find
          for our arrogance, our contrariness, our bloodthirsty history,
          our pitiable play at music, at painting, at letters,
except He be, in some absent-minded way, a fancier of cats, and
          want to keep us,
proud as we are, scratchy as we may be, difficult to tame,
          and yet somehow amusing,
held in His hand, as I have held my cat.

SPAYING

We call it kind, for her kind's sake,
but serve ourselves who cannot bear
to drown kittens, nor suffer strays'
suffering in our secured
towns. We have lost that grace,
pounce, risk, that preens in sun
and blood, breeds, feeds, doing
good in a good field. Nervous,
we pencil in our own names
on lists of endangered species and scramble
to crossbreed: all our lust is steel.
Spayed cats sit in our parlors
as fat and sluggish as we, and blink
or doze through the television evening's
pitch for death and sentiment.

GLASS EXHIBIT: OLD STURBRIDGE VILLAGE

A glass cane, elegant, fragile, useless—
a day's-end whimsey from the molten glass
left after serious jugs, goblets, bowls
and from the breath left over and spirit left.
Paperweights, hand-coolers, laundry pens
might, one supposes, exhaust the maker's impulse,
but down in the lungs there is always residual air
and back in the mind some static. So they worked,
played at work a few minutes more and made
glass trumpets, abstract series of joined bubbles,
all manner of physical babble, baubles,
extrusions from the lumps we are to intricate
creatures we might have been . . .
                                        That atelier
produced flamingos, platypuses, elk,
spider, squid, tortoise, mole, dugong,
elephant and newt in the afternoon
when light and attention scattered to lush purples
that beckon at unreachable horizons.

Sooner or later, we will depart, but whimsey
keeps us at the bench a little longer,
to fool around, to make perhaps some trifle
worth taking along, or leaving behind.

THE SHOP OF HAJI BABA: JERUSALEM

What does the Better Business Bureau know?
The borax artist in his silky suit
lives by the bait-and-switch. But we all do,
who have dreamed of lives as glossy as the ads
and then found out the cost. The loss-leaders
are long gone, to believers, to fanatics
who stood all night in the snow for the door-buster bargains,
and nothing is left but reality, which costs.
The Chamber of Commerce, the Federal Trade Commission,
Nader, Consumers Union—innocents all,
hopeless as annuals stuck in the Shoppers' Mall.
Back in the bazaars in the old city
shopping is serious, offer and counteroffer,
feints, hints, inflections. The dreams of youth
are bartered away, glimmer by golden glimmer,
as we place a value on the world of fact
and learn to settle.
                    Our friend warned us
how sharp, how smooth, how tricky the shopkeeper was,
and yet he had exquisite pieces. We went together
and our friend talked for us, in the back room,
beyond the fakes and the junk set out for tourists,
where they keep the real things in an old-fashioned safe.
It's a little place on the Via Dolorosa.

CLAM DIGGING

Haft rimed with salt, teeth bent
like an old salt's, its wire basket battered,
the clam rake lounges against the barn wall
as codgers will, and waits in the watery sun
for low tide and for me, dreaming of muck,
the Sunday morning grope in the old bed.
Rocks we get, old bolts, sea lettuce, mudders,
and sometimes quahogs. Throwing the rake out,
bracing it on my shoulder, bearing down,
hauling back, hip deep in cold water,
my feet in the ooze, I feel my toes go stone.
It's tough work, but I do little work,
have many toys but only a few tools,
play at work. There would be honor in it
if I were hungry. The harbor's pleasure boats,
seaworthy though they be, make frivolous
flap of their halyards, cluck at the honest smacks
with old snow tires fishermen use as fenders
hung from their hulls. Are there natives and summer people
everywhere in the world? I heave and haul;
my shoulders and arms ache; I cut my hands
opening shellfish; my fountain pen will balk
in my bandaged fingers tomorrow. I do not belong.
Clams are excuses. I dig in the mud with a rake,
hunt for a natural self, look for a life.
The water, clear where I waded in, turns dark,
turns black. Minnows scud, shunning my stain.
I labor on, greedy to fill my bucket
with grace, with bounty, but willing to settle for clams.

SUCCOTASH

Who carried the bean from distant Peru
north to "the Bay of the Small Cape"
where Narragansett waters wash
into the sound to mix, as the kernels
of corn were mixed for succotash?

Misickquatash? Arrant nonsense!
Sooner believe the House of Jacob
invented the dish for the harvest feast
of Tabernacles (Succot-hash),
and the recipe drifted out of the East . . .

Not true, but lexicographers
balk at the clear conclusion, deny
the majesty of the majuscule
for the lima bean (Airedale, for instance,
is always up, by the same rule—

a sense of place, a history).
Proprietary, proper nouns
are monuments, even to food.
My lawyer told me once, "A million,
even of lima beans, is good."

I should have insisted on Lima beans.
Vergilius Maro tells us how
two scholars of Toulouse took knives
to fight about the frequentative
of *esse*. So we spend our lives.

I live, now, across from a graveyard,
armed with a book. How else can one conjure
or placate ghosts who feel in their graves
the weathering of their stones? The spirit
blurs to extinction; the letter saves.

LETTER TO MY SON, AT SCHOOL

Her kidneys gone, her fibrous lungs a disaster,
her heart enlarged, old, oh old and sick,
still she has scampered ahead to meet that master
whose implacable hand we all must learn to lick . . .

No! Too sentimental, too anthropomorphic.
But what else is there? That flesh, sleek, quick,
fails! Chew on that, as she chewed her bone,
worrying at it hour on end: she's gone.

AIRFIELD RABBITS

Beyond the fence, in a dream of endless green
acre on succulent acre, a rabbit heaven—
not a single predator anywhere!—the lean
cottontail rejoices. But nothing is given
without a price. Remember the country mouse,
that innocent our innocence could follow
among the goodies and dangers of that grand house?
The stories are tougher our children learn to swallow.

These airfield rabbits, for instance, discover one night
the grass among the runways and feast away
until a plane takes off, and ears that could sense
the beating wings of a snowy owl in flight
fill with jet-roar, break. Deaf, they stay
the rest of their lives. They can never recross that fence.

TROPICAL FISH

The giant gouramis, the clown loaches put up
with the tank's limits, pretend the plastic plants
real, the gravel natural, and bubble
thanks for the flaked insects we pinch out.
Filtering filtered water through their gills,
they swim through their fourteen gallons and imagine
an infinite world, or turn, dart, and shake
the dream pool of their native Borneo
to reach the clarity of fish-eyed truth:
that this is what there is, is where it is.

Yes, but the red-tailed shark would not, could not.
Refined, delicate, he refused. The gaudy
tail faded to pink; his stomach turned
up; and he drifted off into stronger currents—
the toilet bowl and sewer of death, and the hope
of open water, the heaven of poor fish.

I know better, know about plumbing, and flush
such foolish thoughts behind me. Fungus, age,
or failure to thrive, they are all bad. Live!
But in my best moods and worst, he swims into mind,
that dandy, that odd fish, the red-tailed shark,
and I am sluggish, tame, and compromised,
persisting in a cloudy life, and mourn
that flash of red that graced our tank and died.

DESERT PLANTS

Nature's outcasts, like slum children, tough,
they have learned to take the heat. On barren ground
from which no other plants could draw enough
to keep alive with, cacti and sage abound,

threatened only by fluky weather, a gulp
of rain they are unprepared for. It does not nourish
but splits open their hearts' frugal pulp.
Like them, we have learned to survive, but not to flourish,

and we are undone by freshets of love, and swell
from thrifty pleasures to richness we cannot bear.
Our spines soften. Others have learned to dwell
in rain forests of passion, have settled there

generations ago, and riot is their nature.
Our modesty tells against us. We revel in rain,
wallow in wetness now, but look to the future,
believing in pleasure less than we do in pain.

LE BABOUINISME

We hung in trees once, and small boys will still
scramble up easy apples and eye the tall
oaks and elms. Our legend of the fall
goes back to that old grove we swarmed until
some tempting possibility on the plain
lured us down. With our opposing thumb,
we hefted a dead branch; we had become
hunters with clubs; and somewhere in the brain
a memory persists, lofty, leafy,
so that we, on a walk now, in a furtive hour,
look up to green sanctuaries, escape
our guilt for a while, and try to imagine beefy
baboons, gentle with vegetarian power,
secure in their grip on a joy we barely ape.

TANAGERS

Scarlet dots the highway,
punctuates the swale as tanagers
die by the thousands.

If these twenty years of good seasons end,
the hybrid grains, as soft as we, will die
in the harder times. Datelines approach,
and the stories of famine come closer to home.
A cool spring: lilacs were late;
azaleas bloomed in mid-June;
and the insects were late, so that tanagers starved,
died like drops of blood in a passion
some primitive Spaniard might have painted.

Nightmares of our indigestion seize us.
Starvling faces press against the windows,
watching us eat.
The maître d'hôtel orders the blinds drawn.
Weep in the *pot de crème*, but the waiter
brings another. The kitchen staff
are tough, drown songbirds in brandy,
scold like jays in the kitchen,
and know how to fend, Visigoth blunt.

I wake to the twitter of birds.
The tanager's song, like a sore-throated robin's,
announces survival. A smaller, hardier flock
gorges its way back. Motes in the eye,
red with their black wings, black tails,
they dart across a field of vision,

hungering questions:
How should I live?
Hide out in the mountains with canned goods?
At night, words on a page;
mornings, birds that wheel in a sky
blank as a page.
Struggle or survive?
I do not trust my head, deplore my appetites,
but go on, go on, go on.

How does it happen? Do they fall from the sky?
Or merely fail to rise up from the ground?
Pick the more obvious fear, avoid the other.

AT NAZARÉ

Prawns mayonnaise, grilled turbot, and a view:
the *plage*, the cliffs, the breakers, a sand bar, spray
thirty feet high. We agreed that it would do,
out of season of course, for a week's stay.

After lunch, we walked a little, and shopped
for those long stocking hats the fishermen wear
or a sweater—but there was a shout and everything stopped.
People ran out to the Avenida to stare

at one of those high-prowed fishing boats coming back,
in trouble in that surf. The men explained
what had gone wrong, what should be done, while the black-
clad women stood there, silent, pained.

Another wave, and the boat very nearly broached.
The men groaned, but the fishwives, long past fear,
screamed at the ocean, their men, their lives, reproached
the men in the boat who could not possibly hear.

Their hands to their faces as if to keep them from breaking,
they poured out waves of rage, stormed, then each
calmed a little. The men in the boat were making
progress. They took their shot and made the beach.

A tractor pulled the boat up. The men came ashore.
The crowd scattered. The men who had risked their lives
for thirty dollars' worth of fish—no more—
hung their nets and gave the catch to their wives

who scaled and gutted the fish in the open-air
market. Knives flashed. There was blood in the gutter.

82

The women's jaws were clenched. Their hands made a prayer
too savage for them—or even for us—to utter

now that the men were back. A prayer or a curse,
for they are joined, mated. Their passion's play
echoes in us, for reasons better and worse:
we learn to bear what we can, then turn away.

POUSADA

An invalid dawn seeps light like yellow bile;
a fevered city stirs. There was a time
when skies were cool blue tiles and morning broke
like a breakfast egg, its yolk tempting our hungers.
In that *pousada,* our window shutters opened
down to a valley, out to the hills beyond,
and the smell of grass mixed with the smell of our coffee.
Bullocks were set in the middle distance, plowing
brown lines in the delicate green. The landscape
looked like a landscape, which is what one learns in cloisters
(the *pousada* once was a cloister)—tastes, faiths,
and the coolness of worked stone with flowers that bloom
into ideas of flowers. We bought postcards,
brought the ideas home . . .
                            But the light changes.
In the evening, I saw the valley draw blankets of shadow
from the distant hills, snuggle down, dream
the dots of light from farmhouses constellations.
In the convent the dreams were fiercer. The small cells,
different from the rest of the body, infected
the valley, the hills, the lands beyond the horizon.
Not even stone could contain that virus. It filters
out, down, still. And the body sickens,
twitches, convulses, hallucinates, admires
sickness, the bearers of sickness—ideas and art.

84

EN CASCADELLAS

This poem, an experiment in automatic writing, seems to have been dictated by Don Felipe Guzano, Honduran pharmacist, political activist, and poet of the Naturista school. His long poem, *Pharmucopia*, was lost in the 1867 flood in which Guzano distinguished himself by his heroism and lost his life.

En cascadellas, la sombra tomba de droppos
tournès la tama çiudad inde pampas
en qui bistieros crepent, con leur todos
occuloaros brilliarant en dampas.

Y puis, el sol extenderès ses òngles,
la grandisísta bista, por pounccram
y reclamas ancora fara junglès
los parochales, rèvenzer en calm.

VISAS

1. PASSPORT APPLICATION: REASON FOR TRIP

Gray water and cold, and the sky severe;
yet could I dismiss these chimney wraiths
and turn away from hearth light upon known objects
to venture out beyond our grammar's reach,
sit in the shade of trees I cannot name,
and try to read aright the wheeling of birds
I have never seen before over cities of strangers—
neither for need nor greed, but out of comfort,
moved by study to leave my study to see
the city of Mars, the city of Alexander,
and the two cities that called themselves The City.

What on earth for? At the best I could hope to return
with the dark truths of time, blood, and ruin,
a prayer of thanks for these square, simple houses,
and to stand again under dark Massachusetts skies
and share out trinkets from Istanbul and from Rome.
But not to go would have been worse, to betray
all our ideas of order, our privileged dreams
of the world as an institution of higher learning,
to admit, among the piled leaves of fall
still in the yard, the bitter dust of falls
we shudder to imagine in Massachusetts.

2. BABEL

No end to the making of books, nor top
to that arrogant tower in Shinar, stricken
by languages. They never finished the city
we dwell in still, ruins piled upon ruins,
barrows, tumuli . . . Declining irregular nouns,
we stammer out the ancient riddle: What
is the good life?
                    Who is left to remember
when the high walls fell, or whether in battle
or in a long peace softened by comforts?
Who remembers where the stone was quarried,
or the craftsmanship of repair? The plans are lost.
Besides, those hordes, stronger than we, crude,
swarmed in long ago, have lived among us
contributing curious idioms to the tongue
so the old question may be posed in new ways,
the changing of style our substitute for answers.
Who is happy? Was there not one left,
an artisan, a helper, hod carrier,
upon that blasted tower who never noticed
the end of toiling, continued himself to toil
long after the others had scattered, climbing
the steps still, deaf perhaps or simple?
Was he happy? Are his descendants happy?
Or mad? Or wise, knowing the limits of wisdom,
living like oxen, chewing the cud of faiths
we have studied into extinction?

Ingilizci
konoşuyor musunuz? Do you speak English?
Yes? No? *Evet? Hayir?* Guidebook
in hand I go to the city, εἰς τὴν πόλιν
(Istanbul), to walk the streets, reduced
to that simplicity, to try to learn
whatever stones can tell me, the old walls,
the gaps in the walls. *Yi gormek istiyorum* . . .
I want to see . . .
                    the city of a thousand years.

3. CASINA VALADIER

Feliciano Scarpellini, having no nose,
gazes, it seems, with sadness at the obelisk
in the Piazza Bucarest. *A destro,*
the Casina Valadier does not
"enjoy the *view from its terrace at sunset,"
but gazes backward, inward, through cracked mirrors
to its sumptuous time: Strauss, Mussolini, Farouk,
and Chiang took bitters on those balconies.
The cats prowl, dwindling now, a remnant,
ruins among the ruins. And rats thrive.
Azaleas nevertheless bloom, and fountains.
A chauffeur polishes somebody's Mercedes.
It's Messalina's hill; glamour and evil
relaxed here, a short walk from the Hassler.
The young and the very old come now, and the light
blazes on my sunglasses while the stone
bench chills my bones. Away, below,

the sprawl of Rome. Height like this ennobles,
allows us grandly to condescend on the shambles,
run hot and cold, and listen to palm fronds
chatter like bones. If Scarpellini's nose
is out of joint and socket, still he endures
the betrayal of what he fought for, whatever it was,
and the comfort of the wicked, and the tourists who come
like us, to look down at all those Roman domes
gleaming in the late afternoon fool's gold.

4. EGYPT

Back home, I find the bagels in Star Market
dyed, for our sins, green   for St. Patrick's Day.
Out of Mitzraim for this? There, hatred
every morning with orange juice and coffee
in the Nile Hilton's free *Egyptian Gazette.*
Out of my window, across the river, the tower—
two million dollars of CIA money, my money,
and Nasser's joke, on them as much as us,
the blind, the barefoot, the poor, who must hate to live,
who feed on hate which is cheaper than food, won't spoil,
and nourishes better than we suppose: of themselves,
of God, or His People, the Jews—no change
after four millennia? The weapons
are better now, but the bullocks turn the same
ridiculous water wheels, and the fellahin
still sweat rivers into the Nile.
"The honor of Egypt, sir," the shopkeeper said,
and all of it was for sale. I was told to say,

if anyone at customs opened my baggage,
they are all copies, fakes. "Stolen from tombs.
I guarantee it, sir," and my traveler's checks
I signed but did not date, so he too could smuggle
dollars out of Egypt. Desperation,
the eleventh plague, is constant. And they deserve it.
I wrote in my notebook after the customs check,
safe in the transit lounge, "And dancing, shake
the dust of this country from off my feet."
It's not so simple. I choke on it still, and spit
bitter truths back on the winds: We are
always at somebody else's expense, believe
always that they are wrong, are all wrong.
To be is to struggle, is to wade erect in blood.
Persian, Greek, Roman, Arab, Turk
hacked their histories into each other's flesh,
and the Gippo has learned, and the gentle Jew. And sandbags
tower over the relics in Cairo's museum,
rightly, for so much death demands more,
is worth more, if anything is worth
anything. And comfort and sweet reason
are the enemies' battering rams and mangonels
at our unguarded walls.
                    Lucky, soft,
and yet I know good fortune, neither to trust it,
nor lose it while it lasts. My wooden pharaoh
could be real, the honor of Egypt. They'll fight,
ought to, have the right to fight. Admit it,
but also admit we pray that they may lose.
Let us not fool ourselves, nor break our teeth
a week from now on stale green bagels.

5. ISTANBUL

Along with the right forearm in its golden gauntlet,
a piece of occipital bone of John the Baptist,
hot off Shaloma's tray: there in Topkapi,
veils enough and lust and beheadings to make
your head spin. It arrived in the portmanteau
of Constantine's mother, and stayed to watch the dance—
the toppling dynasties down through the Paleologues,
the dervish whirl of the Sultans' extravagance
on gold divans set with hundreds of rubies.
Can emeralds weigh three pounds, five, seven,
be hollowed out like alabaster for lamps?
Garish, extreme, as any rude tribe would be,
suddenly come to wealth and power, they knew
how even the strongest wall may be breached, the tallest
tower burnt out, starved out, a thousand years
snuffed out in an afternoon, and for good reason
lived like pigs, wallowing in the moment,
time's tub, in which to baptize John
with attar of roses, oil of jasmine, of lotus,
a whiff of something better than the stews
in which most men simmer. The sea, the desert,
the tops of mountains are pure, and, sure, the air
is wonderfully sweet because no men live there. And death
is always the dream of fanatics. Cities, all cities,
all great cities stink, are noisy and bloody.
Five hundred lambs roasted every night
in those kitchens across the courtyard of a palace
built like the tent cities of men on the move,

of fighting men, but stone—to suggest a truce
on good terms, for there is no victory,
and always beyond the walls, on the plains, in the mountains,
some lord, some podesta or voyovod,
draws in the dirt with a stick and would write ruin
in the earth we tread in our ever so elegant slippers.
The kingdom of heaven is always at hand; this kingdom
is always threatened; and honey and locusts are better
than sand. There is always wrath. The trick is to live
in its shadow, to sport daggers set with huge stones
in hilt and scabbard until the day we must fight,
fight to the death to keep what we have seized—
even the relic of that defeatist.
                              The wave
is always the wave of the moment, nor rises in power
jeweled in foam and sunlight to crest, to shine,
except for the shore on which it knows it must fall.

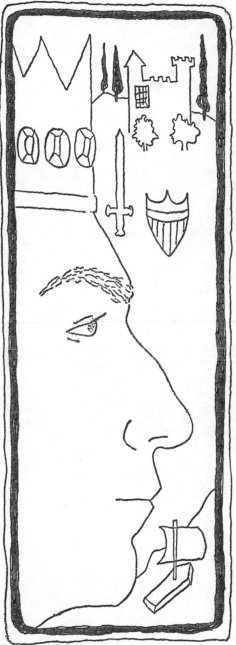

III
TOUGH
CHARACTERS

HADRIAN

Great Louis acted; Gustav built a theater
(where still he plays *Un Ballo in Maschera*) ;
Frederick the Great wrote music; and Henry VIII
worked up a couple of pieces—love songs of course.
But kings have seldom messed with poems.
                                    Madness—
Ludwig, George III, idiot Carlos—
but not this odd ailment. David's psalms,
Solomon's songs, and then a long silence.
The pen on the elegant desk is a serious tool,
the true scepter, fit for edicts, warrants,
dooms—which are also creative writing.
                                    Florus
spoke the truth, did not want to be Caesar,
would not exchange his talent for Hadrian's power.
But what about Hadrian's talent? Yes, he wrote,
the poet-emperor . . . Read the couple of pages
of passable verse that survives: an answer to Florus,
an epitaph, a nice farewell to his soul.
But get it right. Imagine yourself in a room,
elegant, full of *objets de vertu*,
books on the shelves, paintings hung on the walls.
You glance at the signatures, and, "Ah, a Hitler!"

Hadrian, too, killed half a million Jews
(back then they did it by hand). Does that change
the poems before us? Does blood on the hands
foul the indifferent pen? Does the soul scar?
Or is there no cost, no point to experience
which is the realm of kingship?

                              The answer to Florus
is graceful and true—that he would not trade, either,
the gold of power for all of the small change
of tavern life. A serious reply
for which of us has not, to students, to parents,
and most of all to ourselves, insisted with reasons
how serious a thing is poetry,
why it is worth, and how it can redeem
a life?

              Hadrian wouldn't have thought such nonsense.
Blessed or cursed with total recall, his own
Boswell, his own Plutarch, he could name
each of the soldiers in those loud legions he'd marched
from Newcastle to Zion. Could he forget
who and what he was?

                              An ornament, then.
A hobby.

              "He writes well for a gentleman,"
Johnson said of Somerville. *He wrote well
for an emperor* is not so faint in praise
as to say *He governed well for a poet.*

                              Stress,
action, messengers arriving at the gallop,
calculation that hobbles the mind's play . . .
Who can resist and survive? Who can refuse
the final blandishment that turns a man
to the cutting tool of his own imagination?
As the lifting of weights and swimming demand of the muscles
contradictory virtues, so do statecraft
and poetry require exclusive talents,
and life is a list of exclusions, of little deaths.

We have all stopped to watch the play of children
who swarm like starlings, like Tartars, and sing like birds
until a bell rings to settle them all,
to call us all to our various appointments.

THE SHIELD OF ARCHILOCHUS

Archilochus threw away his shield
and left it on the battlefield
with the honor of the Spartan nation
to be picked up by some rude Thracian.
Poets often run away
to live to write another day,
as he did, publishing his verse:
"I'll get another shield, no worse."

The Spartans thought the poem was
of insufficient *dignitas,*
banished him, and arranged his murder,
making the poem much absurder
and giving it a mordant twist
Archilochus, the ironist
could not endorse nor could disclaim.
He lies in the earth with a hero's fame:

Brave on the field of the world's violence,
he threw away the shield of silence.

THE CALF AND THE OX

(XXXVI—The Fables of Avianus)

Scampering the pasture, that's how now,
the brown cow, a calf still, sees
in the next field, yoked to a heavy plow,
the dumb ox, and stops to shoot the breeze:
"What's that contraption? What kind of life
is that?" The questions, even the mocking laugh
get no rise from the ox, but a silent stare
at the farmer who carries a glittering butcher knife
and a light halter, coming toward the calf.
Nobody gets to choose which yoke to wear.

THE TWO COMPANIONS AND THE BEAR

(IX—The Fables of Avianus)

The road dark, the country wild, the pair
already terrified, the hungry bear
was more than a mere projection of their mood,
but shaggy with lumbering life and out for blood.
One of the travelers, lucky or quick, ascended
a tree, but the other, alone after what his friend did,
collapsed on the spot, played possum, became a ball
of helpless flesh desiring to be small.
The bear approached and with an inquiring nose
poked at his obstinate bulk, while his blood froze.
It hesitated. No bear wants to eat
carrion, after all. With one of its feet
it prodded the quondam tidbit, and then went off.
From up in the tree, a tactful, inquiring cough,
and: "You all right?"
                    The blood thawed and flowed,
and the supine fellow picked himself up from the road.
"A hell of a thing," said the one coming down from the tree.
"It was," said the other. "You know what the bear said to me?"
"It *said?* It spoke? What did it say?"
                              "To end
my association with you, you no-good, son-of-a-bitch, piss-ant
        bastard excuse for a friend."

FROM THE DIARIES OF DR. JOHNSON

The glowworm in the garden made complaint
that the candle in the palace window shone
more brilliantly that evening than his own
   light which was faint.

He glimmered in the darkness and in doubt,
but a companion glowworm said, "Just wait!
A candle that can burn at such a rate
   must soon go out."

Had the glowworm only known that in the palace
there were dozens of candles, hundreds, and, if required,
thousands more from the chandler, he'd have expired,
   burning with malice.

Or even, one to one, what was he to feel,
what satisfaction, when the room went dark,
had he suspected that, next day, another spark
   of flint on steel

would make it burn again? They're all bad—
comparisons, envy, pride, invidious vying.
There's a tale of a lightning bug that died, trying
   to glow in plaid.

And yet the companion was right to speak so to his friend.
Nonsense we can live with is better than truth.
Beauty, wealth, talent, vigor, youth
   all come to an end,

and if there is some palace conveniently by,
let us imagine calamities, suffering, woe,
whatever will help us outside, where we know we glow
   faintly and die.

STATYLLIUS FLACCUS RIDES AGAIN

His mule dead, back from another bust,
a prospector carried a halter to Hangman's Hill,
looking to end it all—and found gold dust
in a saddlebag. Finders keepers! Kill
himself? What for? He left the halter there.

One man's hope is another man's despair.
The fellow who'd left the gold came back. It was gone.
Nothing but that beat-up halter. Shit!
We found him later. He'd hung the halter on
a cottonwood and hanged himself from it.

HATRED

In children it burns like tinder, flaring up
for little cause or none in instant dislike
of a schoolmate or a teacher, but it burns out.
Older we hate more carefully, accustomed
to disappointment, rudeness, lies, wrongs,
an adversary world. A waste of effort!
And yet we envy the spendthrift spirits who nurse
like hothouse plants grudges which sometimes bloom
gaudily into revenge.
           And Nebuchadnezzar
hated Hiram the proud king of Tyre,
not only ground his teeth hating, not only
dreamed hating, as anyone might, but waited
years hating all the time. Endurance
is half the art. (Imagine yourself with a sword,
one of those old two-handed brutes, heavy,
hard to hold high, and the man or woman
you hated most ten years ago before you,
bound, kneeling. Pleading. Will you strike?)
When Nebuchadnezzar conquered the city of Tyre,
took proud Hiram captive, and led him home—
of course, in chains—to the city of Babylon,
it blossomed.
           There have been other slow deaths.
Barbarians love them, and the civilized revert
at moments of distraction, but Nebuchadnezzar,
son of Nebopolassar, of Babylon, King,
called for his surgeon and summoned the royal chef,

the former to slice from the captive pieces of flesh
he ordered the latter to prepare for Hiram
to swallow—as the saying goes—his pride.
To starve to death is difficult enough,
but to starve with dainties ever set before one,
minced flesh, marinated in wine,
elegantly spiced, and perfectly cooked . . .
He survived, auto-cannibalizing, for months.

We turn away from what we cannot bear,
leave the dungeon and try to join the court,
to stand near Nebuchadnezzar . . .
                                    We cannot.
Unless we be children again, with royal whims
as absolute as his, to love and hate
past sense, past self, past sanity, we cannot.
Trimming along the corridors of the castle
we stop our ears against the terrible sounds
that float from the dungeon up and the throne room down.

CAMBYSES AND THE CONQUEST OF EGYPT

There are all kinds of defeats—shameful, bloody,
honorable. Victory is always
the same, better. And best of all is peace
as there was with Amasis, king of the prosperous years.
It never rains in Thebes, but when Amasis died
there were droplets. A marvel. Tears? But not for him.
For his son, Psammenitus, and perhaps for Egypt.
The river had been kind, and Egypt had thrived,
gleamed like a jewel in the sun, and flashed its light
into the green eyes of Cambyses, King
of Babylon, King of Lands.
                            He marched south,
the son of Cyrus, to finish the work of Cyrus,
to conquer the last land, Psammenitus' Egypt,
and enclose within the circlet of his crown
the whole world.
                  The battle was very quick,
efficient, even gentle. Cambyses had learned
that Egyptians revere cats and dogs as gods,
see them as Bastat and Anubis,
will never kill them. He rounded up cats and dogs,
all he could find, emptied pounds, grabbed strays,
and drove the animals out in front of his army
toward the Egyptians—who would not hurl a spear
or shoot an arrow, had no choice but to flee
to Memphis. Cambyses followed and laid siege.
    New to the business of warfare, new to the throne,
inexperienced, angry, Psammenitus

did not give to Cambyses' herald the honor
or even the safety heralds ought to have,
acted badly, burned the ship, killed all,
crew and herald too. Stupid, of course.
One ought to aim rage better. Humiliation
is no excuse, nor even injustice. Conquests
do not require, nor can defeats afford
the death of heralds. Psammenitus, Memphis fell . . .
    Cambyses, Herodotus tells us, "resolved to try
the spirit of Psammenitus." It's bad
when novices meet. Cambyses was new too.
Emotion clouds the mind. Statecraft, war,
which ought to be arts, turn into schoolboys' feuds.
Death is enough without unpleasantness.
    Psammenitus was summoned to a parade—
Cambyses watched as Psammenitus watched his daughter
march off with the other girls to be sold
(ten for every man on the herald's ship).
Cambyses was silent. Psammenitus was silent.
Not even a change of expression. More parade,
the young men with the ropes about their necks
and bridles in their mouths (again, ten
for each of the men on the herald's ship) to be killed.
Among them Psammenitus' son.
                              Cambyses watched
Psammenitus watch, mute. The other Egyptians
wept, groaned, cried for mercy. Not he.
    Partly disappointed, partly impressed,
Cambyses went in from the heat. Later that day
he heard about the beggar, some old man

from the court of Amasis, going about for alms,
catching Psammenitus' eye, and provoking at last
tears that fell as from dry skies over Thebes.
Provoking or excusing? He sent to ask.
They brought Psammenitus into the presence to answer.
        "My own misfortunes," he said, "were too great for tears;
but the woe of a friend deserved them. That old man,
rich and strong once, is old and poor,
is Egypt. Son of Cyrus, I weep for him."
        Nice? Neat? Cambyses was taken with it.
He pardoned Psammenitus, sent word that the son
was not to be killed. A messenger rode off
too late—the youngster had been hacked in pieces.
Still, Cambyses had tried. Psammenitus
went free. It wasn't perfect, but one must try
to make do. Psammenitus kept trying,
tried to raise a revolt, raise an army.
He was not successful. Cambyses, older now,
went by the book. Bored, he sentenced the man
to drink bull's blood—it clots and the prisoner chokes,
dies disgusted. Psammenitus' last words
are not recorded. Cambyses didn't care,
had more important things to do, had grown up.

THE BATTLE FOR THYREA

The world is full of crazies. In every village
you find them—an old woman who talks to herself,
or a poor old bastard who, for no reason,
erupts into savage gestures, raves, and subsides.
Barbarians are weird and perhaps crazy
doing the strange things they do. The Scythians
do not appear to be what you would call normal.
But Lacedaemonians, man, are Greeks, like us,
southern, crew-cut, yes, but civilized.
But if they are sane and that's how men should think,
should behave, can behave, then we have problems.

       Thyrea is not very much of an island,
which is why they figured out that peculiar battle.
It wasn't worth a lot of anyone's blood,
theirs or ours. Everybody agreed:
both sides would withdraw, and to settle the question
three hundred Argives and three hundred Spartans would stay—
still more than that piece of rock was worth—
and fight it out. It took a couple of days.
We had to pick our men and count theirs,
and they had to pick and count, and the generals met
to work out the route of retreat for the main body
of both troops so each could see the other
and it all would be fair . . .
                Fair? It was a game
with Thyrea as the trophy, except for the men,
the six hundred left to fight to the death
for Argive honor, for Lacedaemonian pride . . .

It's all madness, maybe, but in the asylum
some are more crazy than others. Six hundred men,
and five hundred and ninety-seven died.
There on that plain that day, in sight of the sea,
with a view across the bay to Thyrea,
our two, Alcanor and Chromius, must have looked
and wondered what the point was. Two Argives
and one Spartan son-of-a-bitch left standing.
It didn't even occur to the two to kill him.
What for? They'd won it. The other, the Spartan,
Othryadas, just stood there, waiting to die,
but neither had the heart. They turned away
to bring to the Argives news of victory.
But the Spartan, still alive, the one man left
on the field of battle, stripped the Argive dead
and carried a pile of armor back to the Spartans,
claiming the victory. The dispute was joined
the next day when both hosts returned
to claim the battle, the island . . . "Two survivors!"
and "Our man was the last, and stripped the bodies,"
the opposing points of argument froze to metal,
sword edge and spear point. This time
instead of hundreds thousands fought and died.

  Absurd but still sane. That Sparta won
is unpleasant perhaps, too neat, and unimportant.
What sticks in the craw is the Lacedaemonian madness.
Othryadas, the survivor, refused to go home,
would not go back to Sparta, and out of shame
at having survived where all his comrades had fallen

killed himself on that already blood-soaked plain.
Of course, they are sick, they are all sick, but here
I tell the story and see in the faces of friends
the admiration, the seeds of an understanding
which may take root and grow, and the mad weeds
will overrun our cultivated patch
and the wild beasts will invade the flocks we have tamed.
Admire that man and the gate stands open;
understand him, and the Lacedaemonians win.

THE SECOND EINSIEDELN ECLOGUE

"Why silent?"
                    Patience will get him to talk,
to start to talk, but then after thirty-eight lines,
it stops. He stops. Only a fragment survives
in the tenth-century codex Hagen found,
the beginnings of two Neronian eclogues, this
and another, perhaps by different hands. Who knows?
          Mystes is troubled, broods. His friend, Glyceranus,
gets him talking. He admits the times are fine,
business is good, there's peace . . .
                              And then, nothing.
We know it, recite it ourselves in the small hours
when will wilts like salad, when normal noises
of wind or a neighborhood cat on the prowl strike dread
of disasters we cannot image and fear the more.
They are only raccoons busy at garbage cans,
but woe snuffles among them for richer prizes.
          He tallies blessings: "Farmers harvest wheat;
herds graze contented; towns prepare
no troops for battle, nor distant wombs nurture
enemies for our children. Apollo rules . . ."
And then nothing. The fire, the plot on Nero . . .
Something bad. It comes sooner or later.
We bear it as we can—the best in silence.

THE GARDEN PATH

Medea, Procne, Klytemnestra,
invite them all to tea.
Their trivial misbehaviors
make no difference to me.

The Greeks were not so special,
deserving such blame, such praise.
Cut-up children or husbands
make plausible canapés.

Stand aside at the door for her,
offer her a chair.
If you notice her hands are dripping blood.
it is not, after all, so rare.

Would she care to walk in the garden?
Hold a parasol over her head,
admire her dress, tell her a story.
If she smiles at you, you're dead.

Look at the top of the fence post. Hush!
A mantis prays in the sun,
a priestess of green violences
with a womanly sense of fun.

The male mantis must surely think so,
approaching. Admire his pluck.
He mounts; she turns and bites his head off.
What's left continues to fuck . . .

I beg your pardon. To copulate.
It's natural. It's life.

Look there, beneath the gazebo step,
a spider approaches his wife.

He has a chance, can mate and survive
if his feet are light on the thread
of her web. Otherwise she strikes and eats him,
body as well as head.

Would she prefer to sit down for a bit?
Does she perhaps feel warm?
The sun burns like a lover's gaze,
and we watch as the bees swarm.

One drone makes it, reaches the queen,
and dies in her embrace.
Falling, he checks his crotch to find
pain and an empty place.

Gone, and the life pours out. Faint,
giddy . . . Does he feel fear?
The light is failing. It's getting cold.
Shall we go in, my dear?

CONSIDERING CATO

The sallies of juvenility glisten
with healthy sweat as syllables leap and vault
or hurl impressive distances. The poets,
  like freshman coaches,

work what they've got but are always recruiting,
scouting the lexical outlands for those odd
gangly naturals. And the aging masters
  seem to do the same,

although the mood is entirely different,
even desperate, as if some *sesame*
might hold open the stone door a while longer,
  and keep away that

hungering darkness all of us must come to.
It's only the middle years when we believe
enough in the world, ourselves, and our talents
  to close up the book

or use it simply to check spellings. The spells
themselves work well enough. It's rather like wine,
with young and old preferring the burgundies
and middle age tending to clarets which ask,
  and give in return,

rather more subtlety. I'm reading Auden;
the old dear appears to have bought it. What words
are *concinnity*, or *eucatastrophe*,
  let alone *pirries*,

to be in poems? I can see it someday,
tires, doctors, and airline pilots willing,
going that route myself. The Onions taste
      is better than none.

Meanwhile, I have been browsing Cato, trying
to play syntax on homily for simple
truths of living which are, I admit, vulgar:
Work hard; honor the masters; mend your fences;
      be kind; hang in there . . .

IN MEMORY OF W. H. AUDEN

(d. 9/28/73)

Not drunk but with a buzz on maybe, he
would have looked odd with carpet slippers (his feet
were bad, his dances mental), come to see
James's grave. He walked up my street.

He wrote that pools of melting snow reflected
clouds, birds, mourners, but he did not
complain that his feet got wet as he inspected
in mud and muddle the Master's simple plot.

He was always good at these poems about the dead—
James, Yeats, his doctor. Now we are left
to say to ourselves for him such words as he said.
But which of us is sufficiently wise or deft?

I have downstairs his photograph a friend
took two years ago. Auden was drunk.
No spirits will raise his spirit now, or mend
the sober afternoon into which we have sunk.

Facility, felicity—his tricks
bested the times, were the little rainbows one
sometimes sees around wrecks in the road's oil slicks . . .
sludge now without his light for sun.

On the opposite page in another obit, I've read
that Mantan Moreland is dead, the Birmingham Brown
chauffeur for Charlie Chan, the man who said,
"Feets, do your stuff," and made his eyes go round.

That fear is what we all feel now, diminished,
unprotected, bereft. Thick in the tongue,
say Auden's dead but the rest of us are finished,
humming in the dark the songs he'd have sung.

A CONCEIT OF LEONIDAS OF TARENTUM

A bearded billy goat (read: us)
nibbled away at some grapevine shoots.
Idly watching, Leonidas
imagined a voice that spoke from the roots:

"Chew, goat, but chew this too:
these roots hold, and I will rise
to produce the libation poured for you
when you shall be trussed for sacrifice."

Neat, mordant, he narrowed his view
to contrive a glimpse of apparent sense.
But look around—it collapses to
a charnel field, grim, immense,

where his epitaph is a proud gloat:
Beneath the sun, Leonidas'
name lives. Perhaps, but the goat
is not impressed that crops the grass.

AFTER AELIAN

Beyond the mountains, out in the wilds,
hunters of animals, living like animals,
dream in the night but not of cities
nor villages, but a plowed field,
a human house with light in the windows,
a boundary, a wall—while we
imagine philosophical marvels
hunkering down to share the meat
and fire of lonely men, suppose
soirees of ultimate refinement.

Consider Aelian's story: a youth,
the lion, the bear, and dog he kept
to keep from going crazy out there,
to pretend listeners when he spoke.
Raised them all from cub and pup,
sharing the food. An outpost, enclave,
cell in the forest of civil peace.
Who has not dreamed that dream, in alley,
bazaar, at home or away from home?
Tired of eating and killing, tired
of watching hunger prey upon hunger,
the young man tried to lift the dark
curtain a little, just once, there.
But then, one day, the dog and the bear . . .

What happened is not clear, cannot be clear.
Perhaps the dog nipped harder than he knew.
Perhaps the bear, swatting back, forgot

he was no more a cub, and in jest, good-natured,
cuffed, ripped the dog open, killed it.
As likely as not, but how could the lion know this?
"Smitten with grief," says Aelian, "filled with the wrath
of right . . ." the lion attacked the bear, mauled it
to a slow death. The story ends with a tag
from Homer on the comfort of friends who avenge.

   Better consider the hunter. What he did
is not recorded, left for us to imagine:
grief, of course, at the death of two companions.
But did he kill the lion for killing the bear?
And had it been grief and rage that moved the lion
or the sight of blood and the whiff of death's perfume?
No way for us to know, or for the youth.
Let us suppose he killed the lion. What then?
Did he just leave the carcasses for vultures?
or skin the bear and eat it?
                              Turn away
deeper into the forest or back to town.
Do not mourn the animals but ourselves,
the raising of that hope, the teasing glimmer
that lurks on our streets and in his mountains,
stalked, stalking still, to savage us all.

120

THE COMPLAINT OF THEODORE PRODROMOS

(floruit 1140)

My father told me, "Son, study!"
believed in it, would bend down
to whisper in my ear: "Over there!
That man's feet were once muddy.
There once were lice upon his gown
bigger than almonds. You want to wear

pointed shoes of expensive kid
like his, wear silk, bathe and smell
of perfumed soaps? Study! Learn!
You must do what that man did,
work as hard and do as well."
He would hold my shoulder, his eyes would burn

bright as the lamp I studied by
for all those years, with pains, with patience.
I did as he told me. I hold degrees—
and nothing else. One cannot buy
bread with declensions and conjugations
or wine with the learning of Socrates.

I peer in my cupboard. A man should see
cheese, sardines, olives, a crust
of bread. I see only lecture notes!
I search my pocket—might a coin be
down near the seams in the pocket-dust?
Pieces of paper, scribbled with quotes.

My poor father! His poor son!
Better had I become an apprentice
to a craftsman—embroiderer or tailor.
I could put the embroidery on
gentlemen's clothes, and be content. Is
this a life? I am weaker, paler

than any apprentice, and older, and curse
in all my learned languages learning.
I pray for coppers, dream of gold.
Study, study! Study my purse.
Learn if these notes might be good for burning.
I am master of hunger, doctor of cold.

AFTER CATULLUS
(LI.a)

The matins of the birds, the panoply
of pink and gold, and the glitter on the grass,
the bustle of traffic, of workmen . . .

                        But I lie sleeping,
The noon sun glares in my morning coffee.
At night the lights burn late, until the bottle
is empty as the talk. This idleness
is exhausting, riotous, wanton, wasting . . .

                              has wasted
kings and the wealthiest cities.
                    "Cut it out!"
you tell me, friend, good friend, my moral surgeon.
I should pick up my head, my pen, and work,
and would but the operation frightens me.
So I hide in bed in the mornings, and drink late,
late into the night, until, too late,
too early, tomorrow has snuck up on us again,
before I was ready, that morrow on which I had counted.

TOUGH CHARACTERS

"Ten things were created on the eve of the Sabbath in the twilight: the mouth of the earth; the mouth of the well; the mouth of the ass; the rainbow; the manna; the rod; the shamir-worm; the shape of the written characters; the writing; and the tables . . ."

—Pirke Abot, V. 9.

You see them exercise; they march in fives
around the prison yard or work in the shops
at tasks we have assigned. We own their lives
or think we do until some mad one stops
short at the cellblock gate, turns, slashes,
and all of them join to riot. They can reduce
our institutions to meat, rubble, ashes.
You watch them always, and wear your side arm loose.

They are not tame, will not do what we say.
Given the chance, they vandalize and kill
as they have always done. On the Sixth Day,
late, as if in afterthought to His will,
the Lord brought forth written characters: they
are savage, with the reek of Chaos still.

EROS

The god seems young, one of the boys
with whom to have a drink, play squash, talk.
His tactful concern, quick understanding are gifts,
and he gives them—freely we think. Good fellow!
But nothing of the kind; unkind, old,
cranky, mad, he believes in himself as Santa
would, delights in punishing our reasonable
pretensions. No cartoon arrows. He slips
powders into our drinks, or maybe he uses
hypnosis. A party trick he does when he's bored,
when the guests are boring, behaving themselves . . . and you
suddenly are an enchantress, and I am a wizard,
and both of us crazy, slavering. You giggle,
blush; I can barely breathe. He sits in a corner,
sips a glass of *retsina*, enjoys himself
and us. A traitor! Pimp! We call him names,
and he nods, smiles, admits that, yes, it's all
done with mirrors. Hurting, I know you hurt,
apologize—for myself and for our friend—
agree it would have been better otherwise,
would have been nice for you and me to be friends,
reach out to touch, to console, but my hand burns
on your skin, from your skin, with his fire.

ZEUS

Stalling above her, failing, falling out,
mastery, the illusion of possession
slipping away, what can the old god do?
Having wrestled women once, he wrestles doubt,
hides on Olympos in thick clouds of depression,
tries to find a hobby, some way to get through
the boring aeons. It does no good to think
of old triumphs with Titans, with girls. The magic
just stops, and, like a stone wall, pink
flesh will yield no more. No more will tragic
beauties like Klytemnestra and Helen appear
to awe mankind. The grip of his lust relaxes.
Immortal and vaguely depressed, he waits to hear
his sacred groves ring with the sound of axes.

126

ODYSSEUS AMONG THE SIRENS

Pleasures we can resist, but truth pulls
harder. A promise of understanding, a vision
of our best selves tugs, the song they sang
while the lines of his plan cut into straining flesh,
drove him crazy or sane as he heard it sound
in the lost places deep in the heart where stores
of lullabies our mothers crooned keep
for our children's comfort or for our own solace.
Who can resist that, would if he could?
        The course was set for home, but a man must live
first in his own body, at home in himself.
Ithaka, worth dying for, was worth
Circe, Calypso, even Nausicaa.
We have met, loved, and left them all, insisting
on our own lives' intentions. Purpose, craft,
achievement steady the helm, cut through swells.
But then by a sudden song they are betrayed.
The question storms: am I worth that wife,
children, home, the world it profiteth not
to gain—a bachelor said—at the cost of my soul?
But husbands, unprepared, hear the summons too
of serious gods, and cry out at the sound
of our own names uttered at night. Shipmates'
ears are always stopped with wax, and their oars
flash as the coast, the opportunity slips,
our lives slip by, the fate that waited years
on a stretch of beach on an unmapped sea, a treasure,
ours alone, that purpose we thought we knew.

Why go farther? What will there be at home
for the hulk, the husk worse than these floating corpses
that litter the beach? Did all of them die? Most?
Only a few? Does it make any difference?
The sirens only sing to me; these others
are nothing, names on a list the fearful recite,
dying of inanition. A girl's voice
licks at my ears, lures, longs for the answer,
that *yes* I can feel well up in my stretched throat.
Can I deny myself? Distrust my body?
Bellow back! Call out, "Oh, my sweet love,
I want, I want . . . We want . . ."
                                    But the squawk of oars
punishing rowlocks mocks us, repeats a taunt
that curdles the air. I limited my gains
to limit my losses. Smart, I outsmarted myself,
became a spectator, and watched my life
shrivel. The beach slips into the past.
          Aft, the wake churns the heart's blood a pink
frothy gold which darkens to rage, then calms
to regret and sentiment. Once out of earshot,
the crew make jokes, offer gestures of comfort
while spray masks the tears unmanly to show,
unmanly not to shed. Crafty Odysseus
considers appearance, knows that if he survives
it will be a point of honor that nobody know
how in the heart something can die, how defeat
defiles, or guess how it will be at home
where a dog, a nurse, a son, and a wife wait
for the lord who will never come: they will all be fooled
by a like, a lesser, a loser, all there is left
of the man who set sail whole, triumphant, from Troy.

SELECTED
POEMS

IV

IDEAS OF
DISORDER

SESTINA FOR THE LAST WEEK OF MARCH

Suddenly the ground is flesh and yielding
as if one walked on a body, and air is breath
and the woods are full of delicate, naked ladies
who hide in bushes and beckon behind the trees
in all the tempting attitudes of abandon
of the famous streets of certain infamous cities.

Who has not heard the erotic promise of cities,
or walked in squares with the light abruptly yielding
to shadows of unimaginable abandon?
But here, in the daylight and fresh air, the breath
of gin hangs on the juniper, and trees
carefully pose themselves like elegant ladies

considering some indiscretion. Ladies
learn to conceal such thoughts in civilized cities.
Oh, sometimes, in a formal park, the trees
will make their improper suggestions, conversation yielding
to difficult silences, the very drawing of breath
becoming absurdly physical: "Abandon

pretense, civilization, cities. Abandon
all the constraints by which you live as ladies.
Strip naked, lie in the grass, pick baby's-breath
bouquets, and flee for your lives, flee the cities . . ."
But they never do. That week of spring yielding
yields itself to summer. Leaves clothe the trees.

And yet, some must have gone. Behind the trees,
those delicate creatures of our fancy's abandon

must have begun somewhere. There are myths yielding
many examples—reasonable ladies
of the kind one meets in fashionable cities
once, in the woods, struggled to catch their breath

and changed in the time it takes to draw a breath,
turning into, melting into trees.
Their stories are embroidered back in the cities,
tamed for us who can bear only so much abandon.
They have been refined, no doubt for the sake of the ladies
who know their truth and long for such a yielding

and for gentlemen of the cities, lest they abandon
fine careers, fine ladies, and run off, yielding
to the whispered breath of nymphs, behind the trees.

ST. PATRICK'S DAY: 47TH STREET

Keep the girl who struts her stuff and twirls
that silver member, surrogate for those
others ranged behind her, keep her off this street.
Abandon Fifth to drumbeats, bagpipe skirls,
and marchers wearing the green. Green, I suppose,
is better than brown, though I've heard the German fleet

refueled sometimes at Ireland. I dislike
these terrors of my mother's childhood playground,
and the drums revive in me her forgotten fears
of the tough micks, as apt to flay a kike
as fly a kite. Massed bugles make a sound
like knives nicking these bearded Jews' old ears

who had, one day in Nuremberg, parades
enough to last them another five thousand years.
They stay indoors with their hoards of precious stones
while green pins, green lies, green fanfaronades
march and admire the marching. Occasional cheers
for the IRA, like moisture, make their bones

ache with rheumatic clairvoyance. Yes, I know
Yeats was a great poet, and the humor of Joyce
is very like Jewish humor. I remember a sign:
CATHOLICS STINK, and my amazement, though
not unmixed with relief that the mad voice
of mobs could cry for other blood than mine.

The Irish (if Australia's the mid-west
of the far-east) are surely the Jews of the north.

But to see them marching in this street is dumb
grief, is the woe of warring at my breast,
is the orange rage I feel, blossoming forth
at the ghettos and post offices in that drum.

SURFERS

The glint of the sun on the water, on bright bodies and bits
      of swimsuit cloth in the blue of the sky
is misleading, for the creatures cannot survive there, need
      air, need food, need warmer temperatures to survive.
It must be some ritual then, or a shared madness,
      or perhaps a cure for a desperate illness,
the worst, the most sorely afflicted, the most desperate
      venturing furthest out
until the nerves, the primitive nerves, confounded
      and numbed by the cold, send lies,
signals of warmth and well-being, back to the brain.
      And they leave,
return to the shore, feeling all right again,
      sporting, euphoric, making characteristic noises,
but then they disappear, presumably inland,
      presumably to die.

DOGS

A pack of dogs, four of them, one of them lame,
and all half-starved and more than half wild. What
do you tell your children? To keep the fences shut!
Those dogs may be dangerous, and yes, it's a shame

their masters have turned them out, you say,
died or disappeared or whatever . . . You call
the Humane Society. It's kinder in a way
than the starvation about to catch them all.

The children are depressed, and later you
are more than depressed. Out in the darkness still
a flashlight beam can pick out the burning eyes
of creatures betrayed. And what is there to do?
We can't even pray any more. The master will
never return. One howls. Another cries.

138

THE ROYAL CANADIAN AIR FORCE EXERCISES

The brave Canadians all leap so
and so many times, run in place,
do their push-ups, sit-ups, grow
ever more fit, step up their pace

as if their achievement levels were rungs
on Jacob's ladder, for it's cold there
and life is meager, physical. Songs
of angels hang in the frosty air

in little puffs. It's not for me!
Better those indolent southern isles
where all one does is lie by the sea
and there aren't any such things as trials

of strength, virtue, endurance, or
of anything but humility. Great
gifts fall down from the heavens for
all—coconuts, sunshine. Inflate

a beach ball—that's my exercise!
The filter pump of the pool provides
an orbit in the reflected skies
in which that gaudy planet rides

till it catches on the steps. Palm trees
chatter over the gentle hum
of the air conditioning. Daiquiris
in December? In January! Come,

let us go where we can believe
that there was an Eden once, and find
a place to endure the fall, to grieve
in moderation for mankind.

MONOMOIT SHARPENING STONE

A stone aspires to smoothness, blooms
in wind and water, gives the rough weather
the polished answer of a perfect face.
But this was a sharpening stone; spears and knives
honed here left scratches. Still, the stone
found kindness in the blades. What is a knife
but the concentration of November wind,
or the idea of a wave, the perfect wave,
wearing its even groove?
Those other scratches, though, crossing the face,
the Indians made, to keep the rock rough,
to keep it useful, keep it what it was,
to wake from its smooth dream this chunk of granite.
Irregularity is fugitive,
must be arrested, even in rocks will run
first smooth, then small, then pebble-light, then sand,
and free, drunk with the wind, giddy, abandoned
to voluptuary transports of the dunes.
But the Indians seized this one, near the water,
convenient to their boats, and made of it
a sharpening stone, keeping it captive, keeping
it honest and itself. The Monomoit
are long gone, now, from Fort Hill and the Cape,
and the stone has been wearing, wearing all the while.
Their traces on it fade; it fades itself,
seduced by the perfection of its smoothness,
the idea of a stone in a hard world.

WEEDING: FLORIDA, JANUARY

for A. Richard Pollock

Under an opulent sun, a *louis d'or*
or ormolu sunburst, riotous, rococo,
hanging like a lavaliere in the sky
over this last bastion of thriving
(have we not heard the news of Atlanta's snow,
the airlift to ice-bound Nantucket?) in bathing trunks,
I am weeding the patio, am rooting out
(*evil* you root out, *corruption, subversion*)
Bermuda grass, nut grass, sage, the grasping
weeds with greedy fingers that clutch topsoil,
reach down to marl and water . . .
                                        To hell with Darwin,
survival of fitness, the idea of the marketplace
of ideas. In this, my *orangerie*,
I will establish my own order, will promote
excellence, pursue grace, till my nails
are black with killing, pinching off opportunity,
maintaining inequality . . .
                                        Like any king,
I know it cannot last, that eventually
the Bermuda grass will send its runners out,
set down its roots, choke out my delicate
favorites. Empires fall. We will grow old,
move out, take an apartment somewhere, and like Windsors
play jacks on a marble table at the Waldorf,
or like that poor Swedish count, in après ski,

kiss hands for dinners.

                    But not yet for a while.

And in the meantime, sweat pours down my chest.
The green corpses pile up. *Je maintiendrai.*

TWO TREES

1.

The willow out back that fell three years ago
hangs on, sends new shoots up along its side,
would rather be a hedge than a tree that died.
And there's an elm stump turned into a low
parody of an elm, a bush, a shrub,
with no uprising trunk, no wineglass grace,
a dwarf among the pitch pine and the scrub-
oaks, a clown, its crown upon its base.

But alive.
            The great Wawona Tunnel Tree,
two millennia old, twenty-three stories tall,
had no such second life, could not choose to be
a sequoia hedge or shrub. It could only fall
as in the empiricists' quandary, unheard, alone
in loud philosophical silence, after which
it became its monument. "We'll let it lie,"
the park superintendent said, and he has shown
good sense. What else to say but, "Son-of-a-bitch!"
that a thing could be so big and still could die?

2.

It could have been a Coca-Cola stand
or a keep-off-the-grass sign some maniac
had left there in the middle of the desert
four days out from anywhere, or a model,
a life-size tree carved out of soap and painted
by a troop of Sahara Boy Scouts—any of these
more probable than a real tree growing there.

144

Most likely, nothing at all, a mirage, perceptions
collecting in hot helmets as water drops
condense on the cold glass of a whiskey soda.
We cannot blame the British soldiers, then,
for discussing among themselves for the five or six minutes
how a tree could be growing there, how it could not grow,
how it had to be an illusion, a trick of the heat,
how they doubted themselves, each other, and the tree.
It is pleasant to let the driver be the youngest,
least certain of himself, least comfortable
with uncertainties, aiming the jeep at the tree,
gunning the motor, pitting his real wheels
against the illusory tree, the ambiguous air,
the deceptive sand, the lying, the unbearable
duplicity of a nature that should be direct
as he had always been taught to try to be.
Laughing, laughing, laughing, and then they hit
the tree.
            Four days out, and there they were
with a wrecked jeep, and the tree in the *Guinness Book
of World Records* as the one farthest away
from any other tree damaged, dying,
and that tough, young scepticism shot to hell:
"It was real. It was there. It was growing out of the scrub
crazier than we were."
                        It is said to be dying,
but nothing is certain. I have also read
that on the Gianicolo, Tasso's blasted oak
after four hundred years has sent out a new shoot.
Close your eyes and Tasso's loony laughter
floats out over the desert like wind, like rain.

BLACK GROUPER AT MARATHON

The sea was a child's drawing, that smooth blue
running out to the ruled horizon, and clear
as so many glasses of it poured patiently
together. On Sunday, perhaps the sea rests too.
Out at the end of the concrete fishing pier
you could look down below the surface and see
the fish nosing the rocks, a mangrove snapper
and others whose names I've never learned. We played
at fishing, not for them but a big old grouper,
dropping the baited hooks down to him. We stayed
for a couple of hours waiting. The sun glazed
that crayoned sea to acrylics and then to a shimmer.
The big black fish on his rounds of the rocks lazed
along, ignoring our invitation to dinner—
which is how he got to be so big, so old.
We wanted all those pounds of his meat, but admired
his craftiness enough to drink to it later.
There was quickness, humor in the schools of mullet, and cold
grace in the barracuda. But that evening, tired,
we talked of survival: there is no virtue greater.

BATH

On the one side, cliffs and a slope down to the river,
placid even above its gentle falls
along the parade garden and colonnade
where swans swim and flowers bloom in November,
and then, on the rise, Squire Allworthy's houses,
the Circus, the Crescents: Bath is a fine town.
But clear away the houses, clear away
the ruins of the baths, the baths themselves,
back to the first mud hole and to Bladud,
the swineherd prince of Cornwall, leprous, banished,
who wallowed like his pigs in this hot mud
and was cured by the mud or sulphur or miracle.
He lived, returned to reign and had an heir.
At these white bones of fascinating fact
Bladud wondered, as at his own, whole flesh,
which he pinched white to watch it turn dream pink,
and each time more amazed, and each new day
a gift, a miracle. He decided that.
The cure was miraculous, or, if natural,
the finding of the spring was miraculous,
and Bladud in that wild west spoke of ease,
the smooth agreement of rough rock and sea,
pink dawns that end the blackest howling night,
and found in every harshness something mild.
He was a despot of benevolence,
a mystic, and to study nature right,
Bladud, in the fullness of his age,

147

healed and holy, reverend Cornish king,
resigned throne, scepter, crown to his son, Leir,
and went to Trinovantum to try again
to fly on the wings of Icarus. Magic, but magic
is making miracles, and Bladud studied magic,
and did rise up a little, high enough
to fall and break that skin he had thought sacred.
The secular bone broke, blood ran, brain splashed
upon Apollo's roof. The sins of fathers
are easier to bear than a father's grace.
And Leir believed his father. His life, too,
he owed to that hot spring that bubbled free
even in winters when the river froze.
It was, his father was, he had to be
exceptional, and therefore he was kind,
a good king, a good father, a good man.
Why not, then, in old age, resign the throne?
Why not believe his daughter Goneril?
Why doubt Cordelia's reticence? Belief,
the moral ether Leir flew through, was higher,
thinner than Trinovantum's air. Bladud
was right about the growling of the sea,
and the wind that cracks its cheeks. They are gentle,
gentler than speeches daughters make.
So Leir fell too.

       Still, in the Pump Room,
the water from the old spring splashes up,
greenish inside a great glass bowl, and tourists
queue to taste the famous curative.

A string ensemble plays. One takes a glass,
catches a tumblerful from one of the spigots,
and tries a sip from Bladud's ancient mud hole.
But people are sensible. Nobody drains the glass.
Whatever the water's power, it is bitter.

HELLBRUN

FOR J. K.

It isn't, but we think of Tivoli
and d'Este's fountains and the way his villa
sits on the hill, commands the waterfall
pouring those millions and millions of gallons down
to slake Lucrezia's little boy's ennui
with the gush of the water organ or the dribble
from shell to shell down the sides of the staircase
that visitors used to climb and tourists still
brave the warnings of the guides to try
weak hearts against Ippolito's hauteur.

It isn't Tivoli. This Sitticus
worked water too, and poured pride on his callers
but with jets in the walls, with fun-house waterspouts
up from the floors, down from the stag horn sprays,
bum-wetting bishops, head-soaking Salzburg burghers
he lured like fish into his grotto nets
of nonsensical bird-noise machines, which water
obscurely ran. Or from the outdoor benches
the fountains now spurt ten feet up in the air
which used to goose his dinner guests who sat
still until he moved, bidet buffoon,
jet jester, and His Eminence, Archbishop.

They meet somewhere. These waggish waterworks
flow into the Salzach and into the sea,
as those so stately fountains fall again
and, slowing through the intricate sluices, flow

150

back into Tivoli's river, and on to the Tiber
which also finds the sea. These fountaineers
were not so far apart. Sitticus' bubble,
designed to keep cut flowers fresh three weeks,
would have delighted d'Este, whose twin mermaids,
their nipples spouting, return the fancied favor.
To disapprove is difficult. That face,
even that foolish face with the running water
inside the head somewhere, filling a cup
and tripping a balance to make the eyes roll back
and tongue stick out in that most common insult,
commands affection—that any man could labor
and lavish love on trivial tricks like this—
and hypnotizes: we listen for the splash,
wait for the awful tongue to repeat its insult,
master the mechanism and learn the rhythm,
to feel the flow of water as a pulse.

This vulgar Sitticus knew the medium,
the water he wrote his name on; the cascade
of questionable jokes must lose their point.
The d'Este crest of eagles and fleurs-de-lis,
worked in stone, is worn away by the water.
Even the finest fountains are temporary.
The splendid spray falls back in self-abuse
to grind the cupidons, the nymphs, the dolphins
smooth again, faceless, nameless, blank as water.
The worst outrages then, for obliteration
must gradually improve the whole effect,
as, here, at Hellbrunn, where the only insult
is in the water, softening the rage
a dead man felt, and we come to feel, drowning.

HARBOR

*O navis, referent in mare te novi
fluctus. O quid agis! fortiter occupa portum.*

—HORACE

Around the point are shallows, the treacherous
sand bars, crazy currents, attention, tense
peering for the channel, gradations in color of the water,
the look of waves, and the easy breath at the mouth
of the harbor, the turning, out of the wind
                                    and into
the look of the city, the rose walls washed
by the late sun, the lines, the roofs' gleaming.
Phoenicians on those fragile craft with sails
like trailing wings and hulls like *gondole*
must have seen cities in such a light, the sea
after, shore forward, promising *tavernas*
and the back street excitements of civilization.

It must be the light, the late wash of the darkening
roses, that corrupts, makes our ports like Tarsus,
like Ephesus, the end of the world seem hours
off at best, and nothing to do for the time
but pass it in a congenial way. And it passes,
and the walls, the beautiful pastel walls, fall
black into the black as black as the wind
keening out there on the spray at the point which
is the end of the world and only waits
to boil in, wash up everything, take all.

THREE IDEAS OF DISORDER

> *". . . on the other hand, we must resist the temptation*
> *to get off cheaply by overusing or otherwise abusing*
> *Rationality of Irrationality strategies."*
>
> —HERMAN KAHN

1. THE WHALES

The whales are in the sound, and sound
of rifle fire as they blow.
Through our opened windows we see no
ragged partisans, gorgeous militiamen, in town,
nothing but morning fog infiltrating darkness. Out
beyond cove and jetty, the whales spout,
a dozen, a score, more, making a noise
of soldiers, of playing at soldiers like small boys.
Still, we are right
to feel the fear, start from our soft sleep,
and stare out toward their noises in the night,
for they are killer whales. They tear and feed
in unimaginable silence, down deep
where the bland green waves above them show
no discoloration, though
their victims bleed and bleed.
Such are the properties they keep.

2. BUILDING, PLANTING, ETC.

Hegel, Hegel, after the tall towers
four blocks high, or ten, after the oblong
balanced buildings, my son has learned the tough

tyranny of blocks. I have watched him struggle
against the lure of symmetry to make
a perfectly stupid building, lovably
unlovely, all projections and truncations,
a mess, splendid and functionless, and have
myself snuck into the playroom, stooped to make
an architectural monster of some kind,
but the irresistible gravity of the blocks
piles up, shows strengths, sensible lines of force.

Alaric entered Rome, you know, determined
to knock it down, knock it all down,
and not just the city either but the empire,
turning it into a tantrum, a rumpus, a pampas . . .
It made no difference. The administrative machine
of undersecretaries and junior clerks
kept on, like the hair and nails of a dead man.

It's hard to do. Bakunin said the urge
to destroy is also a creative urge. It's hard.

Do you know how to plant hyacinth bulbs and jonquils,
the only sane way to get them not
in those arbitrary rows, not in patterns,
not in any order, but perfectly stupid
and natural as flowers ought to be?
Close your eyes, throw, and where they land,
dig.

3. THE POND

The pond is blind. Spring-fed, it goes nowhere
but up and out and into the sun and air.

There are fish in it, but nobody knows how the devil
they got there. It must have connected once with something,
but there's no other water for miles. Alone, odd,
bubbling up of itself and self-containing,
it adorns the pine woods like a jewel in the navel
of a sleeping dancer, or the forehead of a god.
The trees shield it from the winds as if they were fond
of it or their own reflections in the pond.

It isn't at any rate a place where one
would expect to find anything like an abandoned gun,
but there it was, down in the black ooze
of the bottom. Politely, the algae had tried to hide
that glinting of the nickel-plate which shone
still, like the cheap questions: Who fired? Who died?
Somebody must have died. You don't just lose
a thirty-two that way, on a pond, alone.
We hefted the gun that someone must have hurled
here, hoping it was the deepest pond in the world.

Deep? In the middle, sixty feet, which is less
than they used to think, imagining bottomlessness
in those little ponds that glaciers scooped out of the ground,
fissures that went down to the molten core
(nickel, isn't it?) at the planet's center.
Old men tell little boys the local lore—
for instance, in this pond once a horse drowned,
crossing the ice too slowly one mild winter,
horse and sleigh, together. There was never a trace
of either. Deep? As the eyes in that boy's face.

It would be easy to imagine some kind of curse
on this deceptive pond, but it would be worse
to tell the truth, that this tranquillity
is exactly what it seems. In the benign
water, horses, revolvers, beer cans wish
to intrude themselves, to take this landscape and sign
it, but they cannot. This silver civility,
like a queen's, distracts itself with little fish;
we can only presume upon it. Scrupulous, fair,
it shows us our own faces reflected there.

PRECAUTIONS

The twin red pennants of gale warnings drooped
in the dead calm air. Alma, the radio said,
was off Atlantic City: still, the harbor
was still and the air. A mosquito looped
in triumph over the wind of his small will
in virtuoso passes about my head.
I hauled the boat ashore. It was heavy labor.
My boots were heavy. Everything was still
as an impasto landscape not yet dry,
or, if reports be true, as Alma's eye.

I stripped the boat, carried the spars to a bluff
above the reach of any tide. Their varnish
soaked up the sun like syrup, and the sweat
poured down my back like syrup. Good enough.
I dug the anchor into the mud and left
the storm to do its worst, thinking the swinish
weekenders whose boats rode light would get
the wrecks they deserved, spars snapped, their craft adrift
in gale force winds to founder. I drove home
to wait for the weather reports, and the weather to come.

That night it rained some, and the wind rose
but only a little. Eight on the black nine,
and still no storm, or storm but out to sea.
Seven on the eight. I went to bed. All those
boats of the careless weekenders survived
an ordinary night. Battered to bits
they should have been, all wrecked, and only mine

secure in a just world. At Nineveh, He
juggled with gourds for Jonah, but what the hell
difference does anything make if all ends well?

Take Noah, with the ark all built, the hold
an incredible zoo, waiting, waiting for rain
which is predicted but never quite appears
and instead follows a low pressure trough, or a cold
front to the Persian Gulf. Or take Lot,
packing, quitting the cities of the plain
to which nothing at all happens. The careers
of these men are dreadful—rage at the world for not
ending at noon for its wickedness as it should.
The wicked are comforted. It corrupts the good.

There's no sense to it. I remember a tree,
a dead pine that a gust of wind blew over
and the way it hit, just a few feet away
from my children. It was out of sight of the sea
but it was the same wind, the same whim
of the wind, and we could feel the earth quiver
as if it were water. The children stopped their play
a moment, then balanced, danced upon the grim
dead threat, delighted. Lord, let me
keep that balance, that equanimity.

PRUNING

If Aphrodite poured the oil of roses
upon dead Hector and over all love, all war,
the spring still brings new eyes, the new leaf buds,
and even to the oldest bush the pruner
must come to thin, to cut back, to make way.
Romaunt, war, tautology, and all
the other roses, yet is a rose compost,
bone meal or hoof-and-horn, and sand, for drainage,
but mainly pruning, cutting back old runners
to channel the sap into the new wood
abundantly for blooms worth all that labor.
And so the idea of roses, to let the children
cut roses for their mother, tend the seedlings,
eat rose hips, taste the fruit, and learn to tell
the Grand'mere Jennies from the Buccaneers,
and, knowing the bush before the burning, read
with prickered fingers some of the rose's poems.

THE CLEARING

The sky clears, as slate shatters
and light pours, sky blue,
through the gray shards, or melts or tatters,
or merely pales. It is anyway too
dramatic, silly, as the rube's rustic
grin, looking up. What does he know?
As much as the city boy, the mystic
faker, the windowbox Wordsworth. No,
it doesn't mean a blessed thing,
no more than dawn does and the east
all lit with pink, or the coming of spring
and the brown gone green. Let us at least
admit to having been up in a plane,
having seen, from the porthole, cloud banks under
which there was in one place rain
and, in another, sunlight. The wonder
is not that a sky should clear, but that we
should still feel, who know these things,
that hope dawns with dawns. It's perversity,
finding life in clearings, in springs.
It's Pavlov and Jung, joking together.

The light returns. Up go the eyes
in silent prayer to a change of weather,
and, if there's any sense, he dies,
right then. Out. And ought to go.
But what does it matter? Let light come
and, vegetables, we start to grow.
Our hearts, like vegetables, are dumb.

ORLEANS WRECKERS

New Bedford's whales were but small fry to these
fishers of men. They hung their hopes in trees,
lights in the darkness, steady or flashing beacons
on moonless nights. It was kindness of a kind,
when waves beat on the shore. Sometimes in a storm
even the sea gets seasick, water weakens,
and wants to come inland to dry. On elm or pine,
a lamp or two hung right worked like a charm.
The channels at least could come up with the wreckers
and from the beach peer back out at the breakers.

Offshore, the captains steered between the grief
of wreckers' lights and that of disbelief
in every light on the chart. (The old chaos
before the seas and firmament were first
torn apart at the break of the third day
seeps back. The Red Sea miracle surely cost
something; think of the miracle reversed
and Israel under sail.) Their ships made way
or drifted as rocks flirted with oak ribs,
and the wreckers watched like spiders in their webs.

But it was worse than that. Imagine flies,
caught and killed, that turn into allies
of the spider and sing like sirens to their brothers.
To the rocks, the tide, the lying lights, add wrecks
of merchantmen that had gone down before,
their hulls new hazards now for all the others.
Drowned masters on their slimy quarterdecks

connived with their new partners on the shore
to ply the salvage trade. About their hulls
they improvised their own crossed bones and skulls.

They have taken over the business, and from the grave
still take ships, salvage cargos and still save
sailors from the weather. Their wrecks are charted
and marked by the Coast Guard. The bell buoys toll
like steeples of whole churches that have gone down,
which is what they want—to finish what they started,
send back the tides from the bottom up over the shoal,
past sandbar, beach, and up into the town
till the channel they tried for runs along Main Street.
And the Cape is losing ground: each year, four feet.

FALL

It must have been this time of year,
mid-September, when apples fall
from the lower boughs of apple trees—
which is reasonable. In the queer
gardens the painters imagine, all
the plants bloom and bear what they please.
The only rule is for large leaves
to cover Adam's loins and Eve's.

But apples ripen now, and as
they ate they may have wondered why
those bottom leaves on the elm had turned
yellow while the maple was
redder than usual. Still, the sky
was its normal blue, and if they discerned
that the nights had seemed perhaps less warm
than previously, they saw no harm.

Often the painters' angels hold
their burning swords aloft in "The Fall
from Grace," or some such title. But
it was worse than that. It just got cold,
the leaves fell off the trees and all
the naked branches pointed at
the naked pair who knew no reason
for the change of mood, the change of season.

What angel could terrify like an oak,
so familiar a tree gone bright with so
abrupt a show of crimson? How

much worse than the obvious thunderstroke
was the quiet indictment by the snow
of their nakedness! We are used to it now,
and only inaccurate painters remember
how we thought before that first September.

EVERGLADES: BIRD WALK
for Jane and Paul

Ground fog at dawn: the glades, like sleepy women,
wake to the softness of bedclothes.
                            A flash of pink
(a roseate spoonbill) or blue (a heron): thoughts
in the early morning mind that cross like birds
and vanish.
                  Where do they go for the rest of the day?
Peculiar country. Needlefish make patterns
on the water's surface, signals of the nerves
we cannot understand in our thick boots,
tramping around with binoculars . . .
                            Invading?
Surely we are much too clumsy for spies.

The sun comes on, comes into its own, warms,
burns the vapor off to leave clear sailing
for turkey vultures and, look! A red-shouldered hawk.
We go for coffee, having seen . . .
                            What?
More than birds. If poets imagine a country
in which the folk songs are their poems, this
feels like the place it could happen. We explore,
with flag in case, looking to settle ourselves.

PLYMOUTH ROCK

Across from a Howard Johnson's and down the street
from Standish Chevrolet, it's there, all right,
that rock on which presumably Pilgrim feet
first hopped from the deck of the *Mayflower*—a sight
to see, or the rock is, anyway. What heart
but beats a little faster for the start
of something? And all the schoolbooks teach
that this was where it began. So tourists come,
not knowing a thing about First Encounter Beach
across the bay, and stare for a while, dumb

with awe, or guilt at its absence, and then get
window or bumper stickers, souvenirs
of their own pilgrimages. And why not forget
about that other landing and fight? It appears
persnickety for a history to begin
with a battle the founding fathers didn't win.
The Indians drove them off easily, and they fled
here, settled here, stayed—which is the point
that Jamestown missed, not to mention Eric the Red,
or the Portuguese fishermen, running their honky-tonk joint

on the Truro dunes. That story is suppressed
because we prefer to derive from the rock its gray
certainties than to romp on the sand. Half-dressed
little sailors and whores in the school's Thanksgiving play
wouldn't be right. Let them be puritan
Aldens and Standishes. Bury it all again
like the dead fish in the maize hole—Squanto's trick.

166

It's good for growth. Turn over the rock now
and God knows what crawly things would make us sick
wriggling out in the light. But I wonder how

it really happened, whether there was a fight
at First Encounter Beach, or Bradford's men
just marched across the Cape, saw a gleam of light,
called out, ran toward it, and discovered the Portuguese den
of iniquity: no Indians but whores
who packed up their pillows and sailed back to the Azores
while the Pilgrims sailed the other way—for each
must have terrified the other. The Pilgrims won—
by default, but they won. And on the Truro beach
in the summer now psychiatrists take the sun.

CAPE COD HOUSE

The builder of this room who had a sense
of grace and gave more than a thought to grandeur,
in the doors' and windows' classic pediments
and moldings of leaves the local plasterer
could hardly have managed, is nearly a century gone,
and all his line is gone. I watch the sun
lower along their lawn, while two quail feed,
peck over the mown grass, theirs and mine.
The sun, red as the legal seal on a deed
at the day's closing, sets on the dotted line.

At night it is easier. Each piece of furniture
I lived with before stakes claim to its corner;
they signal familiarity with each other
while I eavesdrop. I am the silent partner.
I have taken title, but have not taken root,
and am taking over, learning foot by foot
to feel the space of the house as a blind man, coming
into a new room, inclines his face
to listen to walls. I study the quirks of the plumbing,
the moods of the shrubs. My nerve endings replace

the cobwebs I knocked down. It grows on me,
takes purchase of my senses. I assume
the scale and line of the house, and of Benjamin Bee,
draftsman and first occupant of this room.
I am his creature, and even know his creator—
some architect in the South whom the Civil War

impressed upon this captivated Yankee.
And so on back, until I understand
what bothered Blake who, though rebelliously,
drew how the calipers melt into God's hand.

MOUSE

1.

Death have I dealt six times;
have flung the trap with sprung
bar behind small skull
(the neck smartly snapped
as the dark gout at the ear
bore witness) down the incinerator;
have with my shoe heel crushed
the trapped skittering still;
have once with a mop handle
mauled a mouse to meat
and done with the mess in a dustpan.
Truce, for the time, with the roaches:
my war now is with mice,
the rattling noise in the broiler,
the droppings I find in the broom closet,
the gray blur, only distinct
in its tail, that darts by the dishwasher
to behind the stove. It is war.
With pleasure I bait the mousetrap,
with glee I trip the lever,
imagining into the thwack
and fragility of the neck,
and carefully on the linoleum
I lay the temptation down.
Six have I killed in a month now.
The last of them seems to be trap-shy.

2.

A week and still he lives,
offends like a frayed cuff
or a gaping hole in the pocket
of the garment of my composure.
I should have thought such hatred
would have to be earned. I have watched
my dog stalking the mouse,
ears cocked and breathing shallow,
her anus tightened, freezing
at the familiar noises,
freely intent on her quarry
and the simple pleasure of killing.
Twice I have seen her lunge,
miss by a breath, and walk off
serene in her sense of the odds
who must beat out the mouse but once.
I am no sportsman about it:
I heard it last night in the oven
and turned on the gas—did not light it
but hoping for asphyxiation
left it to hiss at my victim,
until I could no longer bear it.

3.

The mouse is dead—not I
but the cleaning woman killed it,
most casually on the counter,
crushing it there with the breadbox
behind which it ran for shelter.
I should have liked to have done it,

not for the satisfaction
of ridding the kitchen of vermin,
nor for any pride of the kill,
though it certainly took some deftness—
but it had become my mouse
living with my hatred.
Now it is no longer with us
and I almost regret its passing—
from which I can draw no moral
saving that cleaning women
should be in attendance always.
Like mice, their occasional presence
disturbs the whole fabric of living.
For my children, the custom of servants
I wish most sincerely, or none
and ease with the mice of the world
with immunity to the diseases
I have always supposed that they carry,
but immunity more to disgust
at swift-footed, naked-tailed rodents
and quick-legged, shiny-backed bugs.

PLANTING CROCUS

I know the violet's faith, the columbine's
ingratitude, have read and remember so
(rosemary's that). Tangled like unpruned vines,
old lines of garden poems choke the garden;
the pollen of weeds from Twickenham, Eden, Arden,
settles on my plot. The man with the hoe
haunts me, that gruesome woman by Greuze taunts.

The crocus is impatience. The mesh sacks
of bulbs bear pictures of next season's blooms,
a chaste blue for the love of his Smilax.
And I know all about him, except how deep,
how far apart to plant, how he will keep,
how rise six months from now from these small tombs,
know nothing of how his onions grow.

I cultivate my garden. Even to say it
takes nerve, but the trowel helps and the smell of the bed
and the scratch of my digging on its rocks of quiet.
My son helps too, dropping bulbs in the holes
and tamping the ground smooth with his small soles.
He is certain the flowers will come, because I have said
they would. And will they? I can only pray.

I have not mentioned to him the old, dead
bulbs of last year. That owner's hope was high
and a few of his tulips came up, handsome blood-red,
but he had planted many more than we got.
I find the rest of them now, beginning to rot.
The impatience of Crocus is nothing at all to my
own to see all the blossoms or some or none.

THE LEMMINGS

Food short against the long days' hunger, sunset
a fatty morsel in the western broth, and sick
of racing the birds and the tides on the sandspit
for bits of edible sea wrack at which to pick,

it seems no more unreasonable one day
to try at last that sea which somewhere reaches
a western landfall where each footfall may
fester with food, where it rolls down the beaches.

Thus their Columbus argues, convincing them,
for who has the strength to discuss or even care?
Slowly, like a tide, they begin to swim
westward in the nobility of despair.

And if they never return, who can say the conclusion
is the obvious drowning it probably all comes to
who has stared for twenty minutes at the horizon
where the herring silver touches the herring blue?

AT ST. TROPEZ

Naked on the Tahiti Plage
beyond the last umbrella cluster, the last
white pedallo, they lie at the end of the beach
or swim in the blue water, continuous gold,

while planes chartered from Ste. Maxime,
at a hundred and fifty feet buzz breasts, behinds,
return and are gone, having brought and taken
the high aesthetic purity of voyeurs

undisturbed by the long glare
that blurs the honest lechery of yachtsmen
anchored opposite, their glasses sweeping the field,
to the abstract love of an ornithologist.

And a man sits with a yellowy Pernod
and stares out at the port at the end of the day,
having seen them lie in the sun on the belly of Europe
all afternoon, the last people on earth.

A GARLAND FOR ST. AGNES ON MY BIRTHDAY

The war goes on. The seven virtues strive
still with the seven sins, but to no conclusion,
in obscure parts of the world where hills' and rivers'
and generalissimos' names are hard to remember,
barbarous and absurd. Elsewhere, the virtues
triumphant and serene arrange themselves
in various coalitions to meet the occasions
of architecture—seven or ten or four,
like parties in Italian cabinets.
But buildings have four walls and naves four vaults
more often than not, and therefore Agnes, Barbara,
Catherine, and Margaret stand in a line together,
representing the triumphs of innocence, of faith,
of intellectual, and of artistic devotion.

I have no saints, but came into the world
under the sign of St. Agnes Hospital
whose triumph over innocence mother feared,
a popish plot to baptize sickly babies.
I thrived, however, and on the eighth day
was circumcised, according to ritual,
mine, and in her hospital. Triumphant,
I hold no grudge against Agnes—her idea,
and what else is she now but an idea,
a floating allegory turned to legend?
To watch and fast on Agnes' eve may hint
husbands in dreams of "azure-lidded sleep,
in blanchèd linen, smooth and lavender'd,"

176

to pray nine times to the moon and fast three times
on three St. Agnes' eves, catch any man.
It has nothing to do with the actual little martyr
who appeared before her parents from the grave,
radiant in glory. An Hebrew Jew,
but how can I not be touched. Even the lamb
was added later: Agnes and *agnus.*
She can have a flock of lambs. And on her day
two lambs are brought to the pope and blessed and shorn
and their wool spun and woven by the sisters
into palls for the primates. Still, my Agnes
can have her pets, her primates and her pope,
but let her keep the *agnus castus,* too,
the twigs Greek matrons strewed their couches with
to celebrate Demeter's festival.
Like Agnes in her catacomb, Proserpine
appeared again, from under the earth. For the dead
to live again, if only in memory,
I'd pray to Agnes, claim her, yield to her.

Italian planes strafed Ethiopian camels
when I was born. The next year Spain began.
I was nearly four when Barcelona fell,
and four and a half when Warsaw was blitzkrieged.
In Sant' Agnese, built by Constantine,
an old mosaic shows her driven by soldiers,
presumably to the place of her death. My time
is Agnes' time. I have seen the pictures
of dead men on the ground, of women weeping
in streets over their corpses, and under the bombs
that still fell.

177

I am nervous with Margaret's faith.
Her pearl, her *gran Margherita*, is the moon,
the gates of heaven, another world: fanatic.
Catherine, intellectual, with her wheel,
and translation to my Sinai, sets me off;
and a *Santa Caterina* is a mantis
and also an old maid on the skinny side.
I am fond of Barbara, the Heliopolitan
to whom was revealed the truth: that a bathroom
should be built with three windows rather than two
in honor of the Trinity. Her father
beheaded her at once with his own two hands,
and was struck down on the spot by thunder and lightning.
Barbara is the architects' patroness,
also of engineers, and protectress from thunder,
and from the lesser thunder, artillery.
I like the fine arts, fear the bombs and shells,
rockets and missiles, and well could warm to her
except for all those others, dead in my time,
not architects nor painters, and not poets
nor anything but millions and innocent.

It is thirty years my name has been in the files
of St. Agnes Hospital, White Plains, N.Y.,
and therefore in the keeping of that saint,
all radiant in glory, and triumphant
over Rome's soldiers and over her own death.

I pray for her, with or without her lamb.

Show mercy to us all, by having been.

178

TELEPHONES

As if the service might someday be restored,
we keep them, still, on our desks or hanging on walls
for our pretense of expectation or for the bored
children who play with them, dialing imagined calls
to each other, to Santa, the FBI, the Lord

knows whom. But the long lines are down and dumb
for good. How else account for the college classes
in their theory and practice, in which the sophomores, numb,
take notes about period phones. The utility passes
and an art form is all there is left to become.

EXHORTATION TO AN ARAB FRIEND
(1965)

At the Pond of Humm, Mohammed named the treasures:
The Book of God, the People, the Household.
Belief must have, as vessel, the believers,
and therefore al-Islam; and God must have
perfection of His pleasure and His will,
His word proclaimed, obeyed, made history,
and therefore tribal pride is sanctified,
and Khalid strikes at Ctesiphon and Merv
as Joshua struck at Jericho. War becomes
jihad, and the pride of blood is a pool of blood
of which a hundredth part would flood the Humm.
So Persia fell to Khalid, and Egypt fell
to Amr, who sent the news back to Umar:
"I shall not describe the city I have captured.
Suffice it to say I have counted four thousand villas,
four thousand baths, four hundred palaces."
Umar gave the messenger bread and dates,
and thanks and praise to God, Alahu akbar!
for the city of Alexander.
                                        All of us prosper.
We build our cities of marble, our cities of gold,
and say of Babylon or Athens or Rome
that surely such splendor must meet with the favor of God,
must prove that favor. Snuggled in His will,
we stride the high towers, but towers fall.
Even Jerusalem fell, our beautiful city,
Solomon's city, Solomon's temple, all

toys of fortune. And you build Baghdad,
three walls, four gates, and the green dome at the hub,
to do the word of God in your round city.
You prospered there, as all the nations once
have prospered, early or late. Your soldiers learned
that camphor was not salt to be used in cooking.
They had never before seen gold, changed gold dinars
for silver dirhams.
                                    We, too, tended sheep,
saw God, and made a kingdom, and we knew
what you were thinking—that there is no other greatness
than God's alone. But heaven is more splendid
than our Jerusalem or your Baghdad.
The glory of those cities was merely our own.
Of the twenty-two thousand rugs of the just Haroun,
count one for prayer, the rest for luxury,
and reckon the cost as you learned the comforts of Persia
and made the clear horizon of the faith
shimmer as through the heat waves in the desert.
The cause became the excuse; in the bazaars
there were spices from India, Malay dies and metals,
honey and fur from Norway, and ivory
and slaves from Africa. Chinoiserie
was fashionable in Baghdad. The excuse
became a pretext.
                            Declare Alahu akbar!
God is great! even when Mongols come
and Holagou Khan, the grandson of Zingis,
stands at the triple wall of the round city.

Mostosem comes out from his harem of seven hundred
to declare that divine decree has raised the throne
of the Abbassid Caliphate. And God is great!
still while the Khan lays siege to the city and storms it,
burns it and rakes its ashes. Islam fell back
to the desert; the hot sun of the true faith.
You learned what we had learned of God and greatness.

And again. There was snow on the ground for a hundred days
before Constantinople, and the earth
froze hard as rock, the rock as cold as metal.
Suliman was dead of indigestion
having eaten at a single meal a kid,
six roasted fowls, seventy pomegranates,
and a prodigy of the grapes of Taref. Dead
and of no help. Omar ben Abdalaziz
succeeded, prayed, was not to be disturbed,
and by his silence was the siege continued.
From the air, Greek fire, Medea's fire, fell
to sear the snow to steam, to boil the bay,
and all were lost of eighteen hundred ships.
In the spring, in a second wave, seven hundred sixty
set out for Constantinople. Five returned.
Among the losses, count the old idea
that through Islam the world would be perfected,
and the pleasure of Allah be done on earth.
That pleasure was defeat, and at Toulouse,
your Zama lost to the Duke of Aquitaine
his life, his army, providence. I know
the shine of dawn, the gray wolf tail in the east

that sweeps the sky, that burnishes to gold,
and in our dawn we lived in God's hand, too,
with miracles, miracles pouring down from heaven.
The burden of that old prosperity
is the memory we keep, that it keep us.

Nothing but from us. The Ifranji knows
nothing of our lightness of breath, the brightness
of our sky, the glare of white sun on our rocks
in the dry air. In the hot, dry wind, the Samun,
the living God has shown Himself like fire,
has revealed to the two of us, who have taught them—
religion as well as poetry, medicine,
philosophy, numbers, and all manner of knowledge,
but not the knowledge written upon our faces,
running in lines from the eyes, in wadis of wisdom,
graven in flesh by light. It was in the desert,
where we looked for water, for dates to keep alive,
He showed Himself to our prophets and to us.
In the light of reason, in the light of our blood kinship,
in the light of that desert sun that made us both,
let us remember Quedubah, how we lived,
the two of us, greatly, in Cordova, in Baghdad,
and in Damascus, and have converse again:
of death, first, the subject at Almagor,
where riflemen, yours and ours, confront each other
across the river. Death, except as a test
of nerve or faith, is not interesting.
We both know that, having lost all count of our dead.
The Greeks, the Romans choked upon our dead.

The Franks hurled themselves upon you, and your dead
were like a wall before Gerusalemme.
There is faith enough to finish us both. We have swarmed
the earth, have died like flies. Exiles or rulers,
it makes no difference. But coming back here, now,
after all those years, should Ishmael and Isaac
repeat, complete, what Cain and Abel started?

ELEGY FOR WALTER STONE

In August of 1959, I interviewed John Hall Wheelock at his home in Easthampton, N.Y., on the occasion of the publication of Poets of Today VI, *which Mr. Wheelock edited and which included the poetry of Messrs. Gene Baro, Donald Finkel, and Walter Stone.*

1.
In the Apache over Hempstead with Finkel's view
of Fuji and the great wave in my hand . . .
But who would pretend to care? And why should Finkel
(not this particular Finkel, but any Finkel)
have a view of Fuji?
                    So I wondered whether
there was a first-rate delicatessen in all Japan.
An odd business this—when the mind takes off
leaving the body's ground, and the old terrain
with height is suddenly strange and unfamiliar,
when woods are smoothed to shrubbery, to lawn,
to plain green as the U.S. on a map,
when a Fuji is smoothed to paint, and paint to print,
and a craggy Finkel to an anonymous voice.
And the last is worst.
                    In London, on a grant
to study Renaissance eschatology,
the late professor and poet, Walter Stone,
committed suicide: an actual man
ground to a sheaf of poems that follow Finkel's
and in their total committment to aesthetics
go his one better, for somewhere, still, in hiding,
in Queens, or perhaps the Bronx, surreptitious, Finkel

munches pastrami on rye (and afterwards
his tongue hunts for the caraway seeds in the teeth),
giving less of a damn for Fuji than, even, I.
Vive le Finkel! Which is exactly the point.

But let me be honest, for I too am a poet,
and the poet, Stone, is survived by a poet, his wife,
Ruth. And by Finkel (not my conceit, but the real
Donald Finkel, who lives and teaches at Bard),
and by his former students,
                              and by three daughters
who ought to despise that rising, the lyric thrust
that can take a man up where he only guesses at Hempstead,
sees something important in a dead Japanese volcano,
writes—as Stone did—stanzas about a spider
so fine he forgets about his daughters and wife,
forgets even himself, and the piece of work
that a man is, speechless and on the earth.

2.

Later: at night: remembering the plane
and the quick trip out to visit John Hall Wheelock.
We savored the horror of it on the porch
and then went in to lunch.
                        Hart Crane
I can understand. Jumping overboard
was, for him, the perfectly fitting gesture,
with all the grief of his failings as a man,
and still a passing insult to his readers
who cared for the wrong and expendable things.

But Stone

envied the angels' monotonous excellence,
their tuning-fork perfection, their effortlessness,
and even perhaps their wings . . .
                                    The weights of the world
he shrugged off him, as if in a moment of pique:
his shoes, for example, in rows on some closet floor;
and his family, and his automobile, and his hairbrush;
and Vassar College itself where the grass grows green
and the laundry washes two thousand bras a week.
The stupid stuff of the world . . .
                                    He renounced it all,
or perhaps it was a kind of an embrace,
to become, after an unpleasant moment of choking
(or do you feel even that? Does the neck snap
like a pretzel stick and the life go out in an instant
without that terrible dwindling?), like a stone,
like a table, a part of that same dumb stuff
(with a frozen smile for the possible play on his name).
Not merely the notion of rest, but to be a part
of the created world, to rot, to change,
to become absolutely chemical, and godly:
this, perhaps, is more the poet's delusion,
fitting the paradoxical turn of the mind
which rejects itself by its own final thought.
Suddenly, there he was, as dead as a door,
and full of the same dignity as the door
in its wonderful knowledge of the real nature of substance.

Or did he wander off in that dark wood
to visit the *malebolges*, where they talk

in terza rima, suddenly convinced . . .
But no!
     Next I'll be calling out the dolphins
and making him into a hapless youth.
                      He died
taking his motive with him, and leaving us
to guess what his question was that had no answer,
and to think, with awe, of a man dead in his prime.

3.
The plane banked to the left and suddenly landed
as gracefully as a sea bird on a rock,
and I stepped out into the forenoon sun
and the salt smell of the wind coming off the ocean,
and felt that slight irrational sense of relief
that the plane had made it all right, and I was standing
there, on the ground, waving to Mr. Wheelock
who had a cab there, waiting. He told me how
he had once refused to go up in a plane with Lindbergh,
and smiled and remarked on the weather as we rode.
Nineteenth century outside and eighteenth in,
his house stands on a rise with a grove of trees
around it. Seventy summers it has been
standing there, with no other house in view,
and seventy summers John Hall Wheelock has lived
through the rooms of his father's house, and over the lawns.
But it is not virtue:
                some of the good die young,
and some live long, and life is a random thing,
and the bus careens indifferently up on the sidewalk,
and the lightning, witless, streaks down into the park,

and the virus floats on the universal air.
It is not virtue, but a lucky chance
to which we attach perhaps too much importance
(and how we despise any quitting while you're ahead).
Wheelock was calm about it—regretful, but calm—
as we talked of Walter Stone, and then moved on
to talk of poetry or old pewter,
but there is no changing of subject at seventy-three,
and all the time he talked in one gentle tone
of the various guises of the one same thing
that a man must learn to gaze at, more and more:
Stone dead, and the poems left behind,
and the poems he would leave himself, and the pewter
and the house his father left, and the afternoon
perceptibly giving way.
                    Never mind how,
and never mind even when. All death is nature's,
whether by germ in the blood or idea in the head,
or sudden mischance in the wasteful order of things.
Gaze fixedly at it, and the distinctions
disappear.
          An unintellectual sadness
and a dumb calm is all I can summon up
for Walter Stone, for Wheelock, for myself,
for the act of imagination in Finkel's Fuji—
for all these sparks struck off by the turning world.

DISCUSSION, BACK HOME

On San Lorenzo's steps we sat down, tired
by then of interesting sacristies, thirsty, our feet
still feeling the Campanile from days before,
and said, "The hell with it, the hell with it all."
And you, old Cosimo, old George W. Medici,
Avrum ben Giovanni knew all about art
including its worth in lire—or time—and bargained
nicely, being lavish but no sucker;
you would have spent our forty minutes here
admiring your grave, and the idea
of going to Viareggio would have been yours.

"Cosi*mos*," he exclaimed, "with an 'S'! Cosi*mo* is the duke,
but the founder Cosi*mos*, *pater patriae*,
we always call Cosi*mos*. My God!" he said,
and gasped that we had left so lightly, wheeling
back to the buffet, and "Ah, Firenze!"
holding aloft the potato salad spoon.

Different ideas of excellence, what men should do
and what they deserve—insisting on that "S"
with his whole professor's heart. His trip, his life
we slighted on those steps. Your Fiesole hat
that you fanned yourself with, made the slightest possible breeze
and we thought of the breeze that the sea must be bringing in
and decided to stop for *gelati*, and then leave, leave
this city of precious tourismo. Cosimo
inside there knew history too: the blue tide
that sweeps the sand smooth each Riviera morning.

190

DAY SAILING

1.

Distance deceives. Novelists mistake
extent for weight, their thicknesses
for acuity. Endurance rarely
endures. Chichester, Bannister,
Sisyphus sweat. Lazier,
I cannot believe that far,
go to no such lengths.
Day sailing in a small catboat in the bay
satisfies me, who have nowhere to go.

What rarity have the Indies now
but famine, cholera and war,
what riches for a new Magellan
or Drake to take from that arduous route?
The Pacific boils with testing;
Atlantis is long sunk.

Still, the mainsheet tugs,
tiller and centerboard purr.
The wind blows the hair

I go sailing.

2.

It is conversation of craft and force,
the wind so, and the sail and rudder so;

it is compromise between the wind
and me, a settling for that bluff, that flagpole,
and tacking back, beating up the wind,
achieving direction out of indirection;

it is balancing, my weight
to windward, heeling to leeward;

it is a triumph, for civilization is
neither writing, nor painting pictures, nor forging metal,
nor breeding animals, nor sowing grain,
but sailing into the wind, sailing to westward,
the knowing, the craft.

The cove at low tide
swarms, gulls and terns,
sandpipers, and crows
pick over the shingle,
small crabs start,
clams squirt, worms
snake in the rich reek
of sea-wrack rot.
The muck smacks soles,
oozes between my toes.

I bring to the hull a cloth, a plank, a stick,
and bring the hull to life, and it brings me
off the shingle, into the narrow channel,
and out into the bay. The fetor fades
to salt. The wind freshens.

I have my craft—a skill, a trade, duplicity,
a small boat.

3.
The intricate maneuvering for the sake
of maneuvering, or to put myself in the sun
for my tan, or out of the sun for fear of burn,

or just to adjust the look of the boat is not
different from our comfortable lives ashore,
neither praiseworthy nor blameworthy,
except that sometimes when a fresh wind comes up
out of nowhere, out of the south, and I
have to head south to the cove, and the spray breaks
over the bow, and the boat slants, riding, riving
the water, comes about sharp, smart, to find
that it is, I am, seaworthy is something.
I am no sailor, but there is no virtue
wholly irrelevant. The seaman with the oar
must find the farmer willing to improvise
some use for what he carries, able to see
it could make do, perhaps, as a winnowing fan.

V
WOMEN AND CHILDREN

LOVE SONG FOR CELLO

The dazzle of violins, the endless *sanglot*
of violas (Oh, to be young again!) . . . They are so
strenuous. I follow the cello's clear
figuring of the patterns, graceful, slow,

even, it seems, about to nod off—but here
the instrument starts to sing the melody, low,
rich in that register, stern, nearly severe.
And then the abstract patterns appear.

We could, if we chose, trace out our design
in that ensemble, and take the cello's cheer:
"At home in the harmonies as I am, the fine
moments of melody still may come to mind,

and all the better . . ." My dear, that lyric line
is intermittent now. Our tones are deep,
but in the mind's ear, cadenzas keep
alive as I hear your breathing, watch you sleep.

THE ENVOYS

As an impetuous spark
departs from the hearth to venture
up through the curious, dark
chimney of the future
and may not be in a hurry
itself, but acting as proxy
or as intermediary
of the fire, diffident, foxy,

so may these flakes and pieces—
nail parings, dandruff, scabs,
eye grains, urine, faeces—
that time, indelicate, grabs
from a man's idea of his body
scatter upon the earth
and introduce us: shoddy
but not yet without all worth.

And, should the dead be risen,
the torment of sinners may be
an absolute Godly precision
that forces each person to see
the actual face of decay
from innocence, from youth,
as the heavens admit, on a ray
of grace, say, a baby tooth.

BIRTHDAY GREETINGS—FOR LYNN

A blank time—the dreams of dawn are shreddy
beyond recall; the light is still coming up,
but sickly, with no color to it; and birds
are making their regular racket. The waking body
drags the reluctant mind in its rude grip.
Thoughts are not yet in sentences. Bare words . . .

The twitter and croak—they used to suggest the wonder
of waking. And then it was love. We always invest
nature with our thoughts. They sound like hunger
this morning. In the mite-ridden red breast
beats a hustler's fast heart. Extrapolate
and we may expect that chatter to sound like a dirge.
But the day comes on. You move. My darling, my mate,
I listen to your breathing, ebb and surge,

and I take courage, take heart, to fight back the fear
of aging, of dying. It is your birthday's dawn . . .
I look at the moon-terrain you have made of the covers
where you keep me company, once more my peer,
my equal in years, and lovely. Let birds on the lawn
chirp what they will, we are still young, still lovers.

THE VOYEUR

True to his vision, he sweats out the long small hours'
vigil with rain soaking through threadbare cloth,
but his eyes burn bright with belief in beauty's powers,
a belief he shares with artist, madman, and moth.
Harmless, and yet we detest him, we who know well
that same magnificent curve he is praying for.
Which of us never stared in some hotel
at the room across, for a moment, a moment more,
to watch her brush her hair . . .
                                        *And will she undress
there at the dressing table?* (Needles of sweat
are much like raindrops.) For what we receive, *yes*,
it is normal only to give thanks and forget.

200

INTELLECTUAL WOMEN

The negligent beauty of intellectual women
can turn a concert hall or gallery
into a garden—those wisps of chestnut hair
loose at the neck arresting as some common
ferns, if they are properly placed, can be.
Not too precise. One wants that casual air.

They are always busy, making the good better,
their children, their communities, their minds,
and have no time for more than a lipstick and comb,
the good tweed skirt, and the gray cashmere sweater—
but you see the lines of the neck, the waist, the behind,
and know there's a body in which someone is at home.

HIGH WIRE ACT

To walk the high wire up there, to be the main
attraction, to risk—like Wallendas, like Iroquois!
The crowd below admires, it thinks you're insane,
but it gazes up at your daring, aspires to joy . . .
And aspiration itself is the first rung.
Oh, pioneer of heights, of deathless daring,
come off it! It's a game for the dumb young.
Look at those ridiculous clothes you're wearing.

It's a hell of an act! Back down in the stands
the trick is still survival—minute to minute,
day to day, and not to go insane.
To get out of bed in the morning, to wash our hands,
and, as if there were some point, some profit in it,
to keep to that fine line between boredom and pain.

202

ON A LADY FROM PHILADELPHIA

Forbearance, she has said, she owes
to vanity and good sense:
in anger or in grief one shows
the face of a decade hence.

A COMPLIMENT UPON A LAUGH

FOR S. P. G.

Properly heard, it floats,
from Catherine's window to break
on crusts of Kremlin snow
or across moats
of Henri's *grands châteaux.*
Oh, it should wake
the light along the royal air
ordered by *plantes jardinières!*
And such lewd laughter
should cheer the desperate throng
as if it were the rallying song
of their better hereafter.
The empress, the mistress, or the queen,
laughing that way, gay but obscene,
alerts the ministers at the fringes
of that fabric that she weaves
so carelessly (lighter than leaves
on one of their ruinous November binges).
And I have heard it from your throat
and offer roars of mobs you've never heard,
rioting out there, clamoring for the vote,
but ready to quiet at your word.
"Yes, they adore you.
There are millions, ma'am, out in the streets
loyal in their devotion for you.
I'd open the window but for the murderous heat . . ."
You smile and turn away.

                    Include
all such histories, so gaudily true
in the tribute which is properly your due
for that improper laugh, so fine, so lewd.

THREE LOVE POEMS

1.

There is an eagle on the ash Yggdrasil
who knows many things,
but not you who are too quick for him,
too cunnning.

Chen-kuan ended the hsiu-ts'ai degree,
so few could obtain it. But no hsiu-ts'ai
could read your moods,
know what to say to you.

Wife, I am dull of wit and thick of tongue.
What chance have I, what hope,
my love, but love of learning
at your hard school?

2.

I have watched you watch him, seen the dance
of your eyes to the hummingbird feet of the airborne Russian,
felt your pulse as the Italian tenor sang
trills on the vein in front of his forehead, and yours.

The dancer goes off with some boy, and the stout tenor
goes back to his countess, somewhere on Central Park South,
while we have coffee and walk five blocks to the car.

I will not tell you they are faithless gallants
while your ear still sings, your eye still dances, riding,
but know I am the danseur, lifting you up,
the tenor to your soprano. Hear my *"Andiamo!"*
a little above the speed limit, driving home.

3.

At absolute zero, time will freeze
because the air will freeze, and all the music
from transmitters will congeal, the notes slow,
falter, float like steelies. And words. And waves.
Emotion: so that the green of lust, and purple
of affection and orange aggressiveness will form
rainbows. Everything will be rock, crystal,
and there will be no vicissitudes
but only continual contemplation of
the moment before, with consciousness and conscience
solid, rock sure. Conditions of spirit
will shine like lavalieres, or not shine
like all the towering slag heaps of De Beers.
Meanwhile, on cold days, I love you more.

UNCLES WIGGLE THEIR EARS

Uncles wiggle their ears and then
nieces screw up their faces to find
those nerves. We laugh, watch the dog perk
one ear as no uncle can.
Try it, stupid. Smart, the mind
will turn away from what won't work.

For six months, every day, I stood
in a lake, ass-deep, with a paralyzed
dog in my arms to pyramid
on that swimming reflex until she could
work her hind legs, and was surprised
that she learned to stand, to walk. She did,

and I suppose with the right kind of deal,
big money up front, some son-of-a-bitch
would teach himself by continual trying
to perk one ear. I try to feel
again, to produce that first little twitch,
can't tell if it's dead or only dying.

Music: sting. And the muse becomes
Sister Kenny. In montage, show
small things growing, green and blurry.
Cut to: Stockholm. A chorus hums
(voice over). You like it? It'll go!
Can the ear come back? I try. I worry.

FAMILY HISTORY

My father feared the Turks. My grandmother
had saved, like old buttons, fears of another
country, and worries a generation late
followed my father along all Bridgeport's dark
streets, with the threat that any moment great
swarms of scimitars from Seaside Park
would leave their trail of dying and of dead.
Nobody else in Connecticut shared his dread,
and he outgrew it, trading his private war
for the Bunker Hill and Malvern and San Juan
he studied in still-standing Bridgeport's classes—
which was the end of that conscript ancestor
the Czar had sent to fight in Turkestan
and die on one of those nameless Caucasian passes.

LUTE

At Town Hall, in February 1965, when Julian Bream came out with a guitar for a second encore after a program of lute and guitar music, members of the audience shouted, "Lute! Lute!" Mr. Bream replied, "It's bad enough with six strings, never mind fourteen."

They are not serious, violins that sway
their hips and flash their naughty, varnished curves,
flirting with light. And lightly do they play.
Better the lute, whose music is the nerves
throbbing in pain and in key. The flesh on the string
pays for each note, as acupuncture scored
for lutenist and lute. In each cut chord,
each of them fights to make the other sing.

There are other cruel instruments. Flutes demand,
like adolescent girls, that drawn-out kiss.
But the lute, keening under the lutenist's hand,
big in the belly, wild and wanton, is
the hardest mistress. What hurt must go unheard
when, like the harpsichord's quills, on the lute's frets
bare fingers pluck out the music? And he gets
Cutting, Dowland, Batcheler, and Byrd.

His forehead furrows, eyebrows rise and fall.
Racked by the phrases, and in their sway, he sways.
The calluses of his long practice gall
as tender as in his first lute-playing days.
Pavane and galliard equally become
flowers he clutches closer to the thorn.

The lute plays only love songs. All songs torn
out of the body itself by its own thrum

are love songs, surely. Man and instrument
play off the painful comfort of keeping mute
against this playing of natural discontent
on the beautiful, globed body of the lute.
What woman can look and listen and not equate
herself with that shape he cradles. Gradually
she feels his pain, its strings, their harmony
in her stretched nerves, beginning to vibrate.

MAQUILLAGE

A tremor of the lash; the porcelain silence
glazes the bathroom tiles and silvers the face
that follows the other in the silvered glass,
and the hand which in most delicate assurance
twitches the gold of the mascara case,
stopping the breathing of both those low-backed bras.

Dumb on the rim of the tub, I watch you stare
your image down, and then appraise it as
a man might try a weapon, slashing air.
That momentary, cerebrated gaze
dissolves reflection, flesh, to leave bare bone
of beauty's calculation. In the cold
of white tile wall, white basin, tub, and bowl
I wait, and you return, and turn. "All done."

LEPIDOPTERAN

All little legged bugs that buzz, that fly,
or silent, sweep by her hair or beat on the screen,
beetle slick, hairy, or furry, terrify

her: but moths most, with wings in a blurred sheen
and butterflies that send her arm-waving and crying.
Of course, it's psychological (Psyche seen

as butterfly, her luminescence flying
out of the heads of the dead. ἡ ψυχὴ
ἀθάνατος—but the legend seems to be dying).

And for her fears, there is little that one can say
who cannot see those bright souls in the air
wing'd from the blessed isles, or the moths' gray

Stygian shades, longing for lights. They bear
all tombstones with them on their pallid wings.
She cries aloud. Her hands cover her hair.

Her butterflies and moths are furious things.

PARTITI DA COTESTI CHE SON MORTI

Unrehearsed, for the love of laughing, her laughter gushed;
the wind pressed her skirt to her thighs for the love of spring;
and there I was, with her, in a laughing springtime,
when the year's first life of blood and kisses rushed.

Full of the devil and heavenly hopeful, I came
with prayers and oaths and offerings—devoted novitiate,
But I learned my love, and she was a hard mistress.
Oh, a schoolgirl can be such a wise old dame.

She returned my smiles. I put my books away,
and loved till my lips were chapped. Then was the time
for notes and whispers. To hell with the old professor!
"Never forget the footnotes," he used to say.

This I remember: she was false as the lunatic sea.
The tide went out and billowed away to God
knows where, with a furious salty goodbye.
On the beach I still find bits of the old debris.

That clip at her throat, gleaming in half light,
hair with lavender scent, a black scarf—
out of my mind! I want no relics. Go
after her. Go, wish her a good night.

SOUP

Backfloat through a music soup
and listen to the vegetables moan,
    the sad yellow carrots,
    the sly black-eyed peas,
and the song of the wicked, wicked gumbo.

Splash down into that blue tureen
and listen to those vegetables moan,
    the wise old celery,
    the poor brown bean,
and the song of the wicked, wicked gumbo.

WISHES

By children's magic, shooting stars become
opportunities, the instant an insistent
demand—but the small wizard finds he is dumb,

has no idea what to wish for, watches good fortune
fall from the sky to vanish in distant fields.
He vows that he will study how to importune

next time, before the birthday candles gutter,
before the first cuckoo's call has faded away.
He will be ready to wish, have will to utter,

will order his mind and keep that order tight.
But it's not so easy. Who can be so knowing
and still believe there is luck in a meteorite?

CHILDREN'S STORY #1

It looks like the cheap illustrations tipped into our minds,
the turreted castle perched on a hilltop, the sky
splotched with those little clouds we might have drawn.
The portcullis rises; the drawbridge winch unwinds,
and out pops the king to announce to his subjects, from high
to lowest degree, his pleasure. The game is on!

For kings are always whimsical; power displays
itself at its grandest, freed of the props of reason.
The citizens listen, ready for any word—
cruel, kindly, or merely insane. He says
hats are henceforward required of all. It is treason
to go uncovered. Yes, of course it's absurd,

but to make it fun, he offers a prize: to the man
or woman or child who shall bring in the largest hat,
half of the kingdom. (Again? But it's perfectly simple,
The tax rates have been fixed to retrieve it. He can
do it often.) Dispersed, they construct their fat
furry hats, wide-brimmed. Some try a wimple

several feet high. The cleverer milliners build
monstrous pieces of headwear supported by cables.
The strongest can scarcely keep one on his head.
We learn to adapt. Our parents, our teachers have filled
our lives with such arbitrariness. At table
we hold our soup spoons so, and always break bread

before we butter it. Why? It's the mad king
inventing our kingdom in his castle's tower . . .

Hats as long as bicycles, high as trees,
hats with moving parts, hats that can sing
(there are birds inside, announcing the quarter hour),
hats that flop over the shoulder and down to the knees

sprout like great mushrooms about the capital city.
The duchess wears a hat that must be supported
by four footmen, holding it up with poles.
The chancellor has a hood attached to the pretty
purple robe of office he's always sported,
calls it a hat, peers out, and speaks from the holes.

By strength or wealth, the clever, the lucky contrive
to deal with their king's impositions. But there are some
less fortunate, bumpkins the guardsman always catches
hatless. He drags them off. We can't all survive.
Out of the palace dungeons at night, there come
terrible screams. We read the names in dispatches

buried in the papers, and try to ignore
the cloth of pain from which all fashion is cut.
On to the celebration, the contest, the prize . . .
The herald raps his stick. In the palace door,
the king is about to judge the huge hats, but . . .
Who is that? A bareheaded boy! All eyes

turn to the shining face of the youth. The king
is furious. The guardsmen raise their lances.
We know he has come to free us, having read
enough of these stories before. The blue eyes bring
a certainty we'd like to feel. The chances
are never good. But see how he holds his head,

looks the king straight in the eye, and makes his claim:
"Mine is the largest hat!" What? The air?
The old invisible-hat-trick? Nothing like that.
He knows the king is an old hand at this game.
"Mine is the largest possible hat." "What? Where?"
He does a headstand: the whole earth is a hat.

It isn't fair! Protests are filed at once.
He makes a mockery of the royal order.
But the king laughs. The chancellor asks for quiet.
The guardsman stands there, looking like a dunce.
The peasant boy from a village out near the border
rights himself . . . And the fair turns into a riot.

The prisoners are freed. They blink in the sun,
while the king is beheaded. The guards are locked in the cells.
The peasant boy is elected leader-for-life.
The calendar is revised. This is Day One
of the New Order. There is much ringing of bells.
And yet, in a month, the old restlessness runs rife.

There are crowds at the palace gate, loitering, waiting
for a new decree, a contest, an edict, a ban.
It always happens. The leader knows it will,
and next time be worse. He has begun creating
new uniforms, new laws. Diversions can
postpone for a while the fit, the fever, the chill.

We know it too, have read it, have seen it all.
We are tougher than crowds once were, and much more
    knowing.

The guards are increased. There are new stern decrees
which do no good. That those who have risen must fall
is true as whiskey—and both keep our hopes going,
although any leader will tell you, hope's the disease.

CHILDREN'S STORY #2

The dragon dead, the city saved,
the promise must be paid the peasant boy
who will have the hand of the princess and half
the king's realm to roam and rule,
the grain fields, the game forests,
the timberlands and trading towns.
The nobles approve and the common people
praise, and after the feasting, the first
nine days debauch, the pair departs
by the west gate—bride and groom
clattering off in the king's coach
to the new holding to make it home.
The tale is told, but life is left
with days to dawdle out, with wine to drink,
smooth silk to wear now rather than roughness.
Lord of the manor must learn manners,
swap crude sword for silverware,
and after dinner do the intricate dances
that please ladies, and learn games
that stake what would buy a good brood sow
on a card's caprice. The months melt,
seasons slip by, cold comes.
Winter gives way again to the warmth
of a young year, but nothing new
is left to learn, to taste, to try . . .
One wine is like another, one love
not so much better or beautiful than the last.
Chew enough and the choicest meat,

so cleverly cooked, turns to cud.
Nothing he does can make much difference;
cruelty, kindness, virtue, vice
seem much the same in a mannered man.
His riches wrap him, his power protects
from all assault, from any man's envy.
  He himself had done the deed
and lived to learn . . . Oh, rue the rust
on the burnt blade! The cleanest kill
fouls itself as time fades it.
Half drunk, he greets the guests in the hall,
smiles the smile that grows to a grimace,
quiet as cancer, sardonic as death.
Who in hell do they think he is,
and how in hell can they sit to supper
in the manor house of a man who knows
the feel of the flames, the twitching tail
that ought to appear again, amazing,
horrifying, harrowing . . . ?

  The best that the beast could have been and brought
was its double-dealing terrible tongue:
the craven cringe at infernal flames;
the pure perish too, but true
heroes earn their endings, harvest
the fire of angels for their own.
Worst is to know what he knows now—
by whichever way, we deserve dragons.

CHILD'S PLAY

Peter Pan flies in through the window.
They ooh and ah delight, surprise,
who do not see the piano wire
or the rigging in the flies.

They may suspect that Tinker Bell
is a light and bells (off, right),
but they suspend their disbelief . . .
How willful is delight.

Who is to tell them, then, that the fairies
are real enough? It's clear
that Captain Hook is a masturbator
and Peter, a raging queer.

"No one must ever touch me," he says,
not knowing why. But we know.
Wendy will be the lost boy's mother.
Peter's refusal to grow

is too specific. It's Masters and Johnson.
At the end of Act Four, it's corn:
"Do you believe in fairies?" They clap.
We smother discomfort with scorn.

But there it is, and true enough
to reach us, to make us squirm,
for if most of the little Peters will grow,
some will remain infirm

fearing the teeth of the crocodile's mouth
(the clock in the tummy? A womb!),

and sweating out Mrs. Darling's prayer
to the night light left in the room.

Peter blows fairy dust on the children;
they fly, straight on till morning.
It's nineteen hundred and four again.
Vienna's a distant warning.

Their mother, nevertheless, is twitchy.
A face at the window? Who?
Who's there? It's gone. But it will be back.
It's me, peering in. It's you.

And it's who we are, and it's what we know,
and it's what the children do not
(thank God) suspect, about Peter, Sir James,
or us in this intricate plot.

CHILDREN'S STORY #3

In the heat of the afternoon, the maharajah,
strolling by the great pool in his garden,
noticed a beetle swimming—or not even swimming
but from time to time still twitching. And he was moved
from interest to pity to take off his gold ring,
reach out his hand and allow the beetle to climb
into the ring to the huge jewel of safety.
Most carefully, he carried the exhausted
insect to a convenient rose-leaf, nudged it
back to its life and left it to recover—
this in the year of the famine, with hundreds dying
every day, eight or ten in the time
he had lavished on that bug. And yet, all day
he felt a glow of virtue, and into the evening.

RIDDLE

The ghost of a cat, less, less than the grin
of the Cheshire, and its perch a dead tree . . .
But there it is, singing its guts out in
what might be a vulgar *trompe l'oeil* of Dali,
for how else could a cat be bound by the hair
of a horse's tail? And such grotesquerie
has been called the devil's art: who else would dare
combine diversities so to make a thing
you want to cradle, finger, and make sing?

MOZART

If Mozart whistled airs *in utero*
or passed the time while he was sucking his bottle
fingering it as practice for the oboe,
you produced sprung rhythms with your rattle,
    babbled in twelve tones your ethereal
serial music, while eating your cereal.

    But it will not work, it will not. You have composed
nothing, play nothing but the phonograph,
and you are five now—nearly five and a half—
who can carry only precariously a tune.
    In the afternoons, when Mr. Mozart dozed,
little Wolfgang used to play the buffoon—

    played the piano I mean: progressions of chords,
incompletely, and the old man had
to get up, bang the tonic, say gruff words
    and then go back to his nap. Pick out the line
of "Jingle Bells," the commercial for Mr. Clean,
and I would bound from your mother's embrace to applaud.

    I had got used to my not being Mozart,
    but in a son's first year what father's heart
has never fluttered once, imagining,
    with little enough reason, despite more . . .
I love you as myself. Badly I sing
a lullaby to your tin ear, heartsore.

JIGSAW PUZZLE

The shapes are irrational, the colors, tricks—
is this cloud or reflection of cloud on the lake?
Putting the pieces together would be a chore
if what you did was put them together, fix
the shattered picture on the box, a fake
École de Paris horror. But you ignore
the picture as beside the point, and teach
the pieces to do the work. You do not reach
for the base of that tree, say, but let it come
of its own will to your hand and to its place.
Your attention attenuates, and in a haze
of peripheral vision you start to see the dumb
cardboard pieces come to life and race
around the bridge table top, aware, ablaze.

TOURING

Architecture, painting, tapisserie . . .
but gore is what we tour. The seriousness
of a nation comes from the seriousness of its crimes;
and we drive for hours to see into what odd shapes
the tongues of old fires have licked châteaux,
cathedrals, or the countryside.
                              The children
climbed on a pillbox at Juno beach. The sun
climbed in the sky. Boats lay up on shore
posing for postcards. Clouds arranged themselves
as if painted there by naïfs. Our bellies rumbled
louder than all the guns of Normandie;
we drove away to see about lunch at Bayeux
and the needlework of William's war with Harold,
reading the *Guide Verte* as we sped along
those terrible hedgerows.
                        Why? For culture of course.
If culture, like power, grew out of the end of a gun,
it would all be simpler. We could take our place
with England, France, Germany, Italy, Spain,
and claim a like seriousness.
                            A dog,
black, half-starved, hunches down in an alley,
trying to pass a worm.
                      We drive away,
knowing that both the dog and the worm will die.
I cannot decide which of them is which—
culture or history. They fit both ways.

The sun that danced gold on the waves of the channel
could, if it chose, bleach those bones to white,
intricate, pure as the vaulting of King's chapel,
and chance, blind, could keep them like a saint's . . .
Not, of course, that we went through all this.
We distracted the children at once. Delicate minds—
delicate stomachs—don't need such truths before lunch.

THE COVENANT

Let the world be wary of my son,
be gentle with him, be reverent—
not for the laughter I love,
nor for his possible *Hamlet* or *Zauberflöte*,
but as their very savior
                              from those glaciers
the ovens turned to slush, from the clouds
that gathered above those chimneys.
Let the world rejoice in him,
its trustee and its signator
whose person is as holy as a king's,
the child-hero, Dutchboy of the dikes:
he keeps the ice caps frozen, the salt sea
splashing in its bed, the clouds moving,
the world safe, at least for another lifetime,
safe, at least for a while, at least from the flood.

TABLEAU À LA ROUSSEAU

That lions like lavender is amiable; for the mane's
tawny to find complement in the green
spike with the sharp accent of the blossom
is not mere whimsey, as delight in catnip
would be, but somehow right. One can nearly
see in those slow yellow eyes a need to express
the innate refinement lions have, and lavender
must be a relief from the flesh-red, blood-red
redness of their usual provender
and the bloody obviousness of crimson with gold.
Or, it may be the odor, or
just to adore such a vegetable vegetable.
It extends the range of lions, even as they
extend its possibilities: they may
love most to patronize, to let it be said
that among the lovers of lavender are lions.

SEALS

The fish
that fly,
dead, flung by
the counting keeper—
more to the sluggish,
fewer to the sleeker
seals—nourish
fairly, filling up
as heaven equally fills
every unequal cup.

To watch
among
them, to favor young
or elderly or sick
seals not up to catching
lunch with a trick
or to fend off the snatching
of the greedier ones requires
a number of different skills
from those the crowd admires.

And so
with seals:
youngsters take meals
in small, separate pools
where keepers throw
smelts, seal schools
where the young grow

clever, and able to compete
with adults for the flung
fish they will have to eat.

To live
in zoos,
the animals lose
natural seal sense,
and being captive,
acquire dependence,
even on imitative
children who throw balls.
The seals oblige and catch
what miscellany falls.

They bark
as they
always do, play
for a while longer,
having made of life a lark
and a game of hunger.
But later, in the dark
a seal will get sick,
get sick to death, fed up
at last with its one trick.

SPECULATIONS ABOUT THE DEATH OF ESKIMOS

I have often imagined the moment—on the white
moonlit ice in the black of polar water,
its erratic pitch and yaw, the wind's bite
and the shapes on shore of son, grandson, granddaughter

still as whalebone, gazing as I go.
I once tried to build an igloo, thought the dogsled
fun—I liked dogs—but the Eskimo,
with his fur-fringed, weather-worn face, filled me with dread,

shipping his relatives off on the ice to die—
to freeze? to starve? to drown? I couldn't decide,
for I was always on that ice floe by
some terrible mistake. On shore, they cried

and were sorry to learn, too late, how much they loved me.
It is not like that at all, but very formal,
undemonstrative, done with some dignity.
Death is not melodramatic but, properly, normal.

And the cause of death is almost certainly freezing,
which is painless, quick, cleaner than razor or pill,
rifle, rope, or guillotine for easing
the last agonies. So gently does cold kill

and so familiar is it to Eskimos
that tears are unlikely indeed. The departure itself
is visibly simple. The strip of water grows
wider and wider between floe and ice shelf;

neither physician nor priest is required to say
which moment is the last; it is perfectly clear
that there he is, slowly drifting away.
Calmly they wait for him to disappear.

And out of sight of the shore, the sting of the cold,
and the sting abating. The feet begin to feel numb.
It happens so slowly; slowly one grows old,
one learns the patience to wait for death to come.

The flab around the middle, the slack skin,
the defeats that flesh has suffered are undone:
the wattles wed again to the firm chin,
the fat is hard as bone, the bone as stone.

That I have changed my mind in twenty years
is reasonable. My fear was a child's fault.
I make my way and that cold shore appears
not unattractive as I start to smell salt.

236

FIRST SNOW

For Sarah

The white is arbitrary. It could have been blue,
falling in blue flakes from the blue sky,
or pink, the color of cold of the bathroom tiles.
But the evenness is impressive, the planes, the too
graded, too smooth yard, street tidied by
this wet, white whim that stretches on for miles.

Footprints, however. She experiments with a boot,
then willful looping about the lawn. She is
all seriousness as, in her red snowsuit,
she stamps along in her anabasis
to civilize this wilderness. Her tracks
make random roads, approximate a town.
She laughs. She sits in the snow. She can relax
and play in it, now that nature has been put down.

F. A. O. SCHWARZ

". . . would needsly scorse,
A costly Jewell for a Hobby-Horse . . ."

—Michael Drayton

More than their children, they too are pretenders
whose tykes on trikes, their sons, they see sun-kings,
and bear them, like ambassadors, such baubles
as Fabergé designed and moneylenders
reckoned in years of taxes. And Schwarz's things
have still that high contempt of a million rubles.

Though crowns be gone, God save the attitude
of the dauphin playing with his cup and ball
as if to dare goddams to shake his throne.
On a four-hundred-dollar horse a diminutive dude
can look dispassionately on the fall
his France is threatened with, and wait for Joan.

"A Jewell for a Hobby-Horse"? The exchange
is better than fair. With the toy's extravagance
they mark the child as the last of royalty
who gallops, careless of their broadloom range,
and, sharing his noble disdain of circumstance
(his kingdom is a horse), swear loyalty.

SOLOMON GRUNDY

A bedtime poem for my son

1.

Pity and terror are not for little boys
who neither want nor need nor can enjoy
the agonies of Job, the blind tears
of Oedipus, or Hamlet sung to rest by angels.
Let us rehearse the tale of a good man
who lived and died in virtue and some fame,
whose tame and common truth is smooth with telling,
yet hard and fast as ever truth was told.

Solomon Grundy was born, thereafter christened,
and married in due course. Some years went by
and Mr. Grundy, husband, Christian, man,
took ill, was worse in sickness, and he died.
His people laid him in earth; his epitaph
was simple: *this is the end of Solomon Grundy.*

2.

We know little of him. Those few events
of which we do have evidence tell nothing.
His life, like Shakespeare's, stands in bas-relief:
birth, christening, marriage, death, and stone.
No evil that he did lives after him,
and yet is remembered. Although no
records tell of any title, office,
commission, honor, real property,
nor court reports make mention of his business,

small children say his rime and bounce a ball
in private rhythms (each of them his end).

Solomon Grundy, born, married and died . . .
his study is the limit of our knowing,
who read ourselves in him: a name in time.

3.
He lived the days of the week that are our days;
his face is with the faces on our mantel
and in our albums, in dated, formal poses,
monuments to our passing.
                Born on Monday,
married and the date engraved in gold . . .
as if, by such devices, we could claim
the date itself, capture the day as ours
on calendars, in almanacs, forever.

Solomon Grundy was buried on Sunday—the children,
all the endless children say it, smiling,
who know the ends of rimes and weeks and men,
simple as that. And mourn for none of them.

4.
Your eyes have closed and at the edge of sleep
you hear my voice, cozy as a blanket,
ramble on in the dark with a grim tale
of sickness and inexorable death
which you find full of symmetry and rhythm
and comforting.
              When Mr. Grundy died,
that Saturday with all his days commingled

like my words now into one afternoon,
a texture on his bed, a monotone,
he knew this was no tale for a little boy
with scenes arranged around a catafalque
showing us mortal men and full of death,
nor for a father, either, whose deep voice
has lost the sing-song tune.
                            But you and I
must meet in the confusion of his sunset
the boundary of time and its own verge.

BALLOONS

Even two years is plenty of downwardness,
the tiresomeness of it, the boring sameness of weight.
That the block with the zebra on it, splendidly flipped
with a speculative off-hand sidearm more or less
toss, should not, even briefly, hesitate
but fall like a sedulous clerk, obedient, whipped

is an outrageous waste of perfectly good possibility.
Imagine, then, this too blue picture postcard
day, with the animals loping or sleeping in sun
and the air not cold but crisp with the civility
of good servants, walking from lions toward
okapis, gnus, giraffes, and coming upon

this not quite picturesque enough person with his
overpriced ice cream, his Cracker Jacks, and for the first
time in one's entire life, balloons which stand
up. Up! A hair cut at Best's is
all one could want, but the balloons they hand out are the worst
droopers and fallers and danglers from one's hand—

But these, most marvelously balanced on their strings,
these beautiful blue zoo hallucinations
of the crew-cut and, alas, un-Italianate vendor
sway with the wind: not mere imaginings
but real things of the real world on vacations
from its gross, gray gravity, or on a bender

with only a single strand left of sobriety
as though they were rid of their shoes, but encumbered by

the still recalcitrant laces. Familiar with jumping
on the big double bed, for example, and filled to satiety
with the creak of springs, the pillows' obesity,
the flatness of mattresses, bathos, the bore of clumping

back down, I bought one of the balloons
green and giddy with gas, and brought it home
to watch it nose the ceiling like a goldfish,
only to see it lose that afternoon's
buoyancy, decline and fall, like Rome,
with that tired grace that is the final wish

of all extravagant high living. Back at the zoo
having felt that sweet tug at my finger,
I should have let it go and lived its flying.
It would have been the humane thing to do.
But you ignore the elephants, don't you, and linger
to share the captive platypus's dying.

BLOCKS

At random playing and by accident,
having set two blocks, the small hands take a third,
place it across—and those two have become
posts and this third suddenly a lintel.
A gate! an arch! a door! An elemental
awe: here, without any bugle or drum,
free of distraction from any chiseled word,
he looks upon the towering monument

to the simple setting of thing on thing: abstract
but undeniable structure. The enclosed space
is charmed, is holy. The hand is held in wonder
and fear of touching that third inviolate
block crowning the simple new-made gate.
The world is divided into an over and under,
and all is in or out. And at this place
all quadrants and divisions meet, exact,

where the marker marks itself, where on the floor
the child, prone, peers through the opening,
fixed on nothing, the nothing at all at the center,
space beneath the one block and between two
(a miracle, he is learning is his due,
like the first summer after the first winter),
no mere and general marveling at the thing
but a corkscrew staring into the empty core.

244

NURSERY RIME

For Joshua

bo
peep
little bo peep
little old bittle old o bo peep

old bo peep
little bo peep
little ittle bo pittle ittle o peep
o o peep
little old peep
bittle ittle odle ittle o bittle peep bo
odle ittle peep bo
little bo peep

hey diddle diddle and a little bo peep
little bo diddle hey little bo peep
fiddle faddle peep hey
bo bo peep hey
little diddle he pay
heap peep peep

bo
peep
little bo peep
had a little ho ho
goodbye peep

VI
INHUMANITIES

WARNING

First, beyond all
song, or any note,
was that terrible small
silence in her lovely throat—
and all along,
the quiet potency for
most fantastic song.

Still, there lingers
in Philomela's cries
the echo of her deft fingers
when her music flies.
She could not sing
except for outraged muteness,
Procne, and the king

who had his wild will.
You, who would make bold,
beware when they keep still.
The tale is old:
quiet as snow,
a heart will burst—then warble
when the mind lets go.

THE SCHOOL OF ATHENS

The barbarous Illyrian, Upranda,
styled himself Justinian. His Greek
was, nonetheless, laughable, fitting only
for adjudication of circus brawls, speeches
in the worst taste (I mean the dedication
of Anthemius' church, that ghastly flat-domed wonder),
and Constantinople U.
                    But this crude mouth
brought an end to the School of Athens, and severed
the golden chain that stretched to the time of Plato
who was no Christer either.
                    Then the professors
Diogenes, Eulalias, Hermias,
Priscian, Damascius, and Isidore
and master Simplicius departed for Persia.

There, it was rumored, existed the Republic:
there was Chosroes, the philosopher king,
and every kind of virtue Socrates
had conjured up in Polemarchus' house.
The huge rubies, the tiger skins from Persia,
the spices, the fabled lushness of vegetation
hinted the excellence of that rare land,
where, with the men, the women were taught gymnastics,
Sicilian cookery was banned, and Corinthian orgies,
and all things were harmonious, and good.

In ships they went, making most perilous voyage,
and across rough country, and dusty and cold,

these elderly professors with their books,
and came at last to Persia.

But the soul
did not order the mind, or the mind the body
in Persia either, but lasciviousness
held sway of government and courtesans
were better loved than logic. Corinth was pure
and the food in Syracuse most plain and wholesome
compared to Persia. There, ignoble nobles,
discourteous courtiers and foolish wise men
amused the king, who was philosopher
of vanity, ambition, cruelty . . .
And the dead were left exposed to the carrion birds.
And brothers married sisters as in Egypt.

They gathered their books again, and wept, and journeyed
back to the Empire's borders and civilization,
to live out their lives in tranquil misery,
agreement having been made in the treaty with Persia:
In consideration of eternal peace,
Justinian shall pay to Chosroes
eleven thousand pounds of gold, shall cede
the right to occupy Dara, shall guarantee
the lives and safety of these philosophers ((named)) . . .
Chosroes ((sigil)) et Upranda ((sigil))
Simplicius died last and with him Athens.

ACTAEON

1.

No nasty Tom, but with loud horns and yelping
in honest hunt, Actaeon in that wood,
come to a clearing, saw the goddess naked,
she and her maidens, laving in a pool—

and still, no light, no multifoliate rose,
nothing of supernature

                but washing women.
"Cognosce dominas tuas!"?

                    "Cave canes!"?

                          Posted?
nothing,
        but rustle of green leaves over them,
and rush of water blue in afternoon
and wet limbs gleaming in the sprinkled sunlight.
So hid he then, the hero in that wood
within a thicket, innocent as they
and gay for the adventure

                      (as Anchises
was with Aphrodite who asked only,
"Do not go bragging at your feasting tables
nor whisper privily in the small hours,
nor tell to any man that, 'Aphrodite
was my Aeneas' dam. I tupped a goddess . . .'"
This he denied and was struck down most sorely.)

and still by Gargaphie's pool was no betrayal,
but only beauty swimming in his eyes.

2.

Granting injustice, we must grant also
the teeth tearing the flesh, the cries of comrades,
where is Actaeon? words (his friends' teeth) snapped
as all rushed to the kill, and grant his death
—more lively than a picture gallery.
for here was no carved marble—a rare find,
who have no beauty for ourselves to die in,
no birdsong loud enough to break the drum.

Hiding in the bush it was mere vision,
until the watersplash, when all her beauty
tickled down his neck. Front to front,
mortal and goddess, bank and pool, wet,
both:
                me miserum dicturus erat.
And we must grant it all, then, knowing nothing,
who sleep through dawns, and who forget death
lurking in sunsets that must be followed boldly.

Allow then passion in the sprouting antlers
where *verba animo desunt;* fear the dogs
running the rough stigmata in their jaws.

3.

He and Diana: considering them, we
must follow with the huntsmen in the chase,
must stand with the attendants in the pool,
witnessing leaves in the wind, the clouds, riding
random in the usual sky, the visible
hills far off, the earth under our feet:
background, understanding background only.

"We cannot even say with a certainty,
'There was something . . . I remember something
in the quiet afternoon . . .'
                          and yet, we saw,
not knowing enough of love to call these 'lovers'
(the burden of miracles is for the observers),
the sudden change: man into mute stag.
Wholly transparent, purer than crystal, invisible,
nothing betrayed them to us. A stately change:
as, by a thought, a bowl on a potter's wheel
becomes a vase—sudden and yet with grace:
as Zeus was a swan, a bull, a golden shower,
Actaeon
           was a stag."

ORPHEUS

Floating his lifeless head, the river ran
that once had shimmered still to his living song,
bobbed it in current, rolled it in running water,
and the head of the charmer, singer, Orpheus, silent
as the death that washed it, suddenly, lively sang.
Then, as a stream of water, a stream of music
coursed through his brains, as blood flowing like crystal.
   I have lived there; have made in my own ghostliness
   Hades, Persephone, 'live in my lyre's moment,
   quicken to melody—performed all this easily
   as I have turned stags into the shades of my music.
The river sang all along out of mouth and source
from the speck in the water to riverbank and wood
and mountains away, ranges of audience heard
the heart in the head, beating its notes out of silence.
The joy of singing sang to the theory of song:
no one to no one, of mathematics and air.
The floating wonder spun along the water
while the trees held still to listen that they could dance.
   My song outlives me, having charmed the furies.
   There is no death, and they will sing it always
   having heard it once. I, I am the singer,
   maker, master. Deathless, I am the song.
His head floated down the river and into the sea
where the currents caught it and carried it to Lesbos
and the waves washed it up on a sandy beach.
And there, covered with brine and caked with sand,
the head of Orpheus, spectacle for sea birds,

lying on its side, bodied by driftwood—
there, still, the head in its spirit sang
prophecies, oracles, far and wild on the winds.
    Real as my music, alive as all that hear me,
    I sing my testament in simple phrases:
    Godless, whatever I choose, I can make immortal,
    unnatural and worldly by my lyre.
There was no body now for head to turn on,
and all the landscape, forward, in it, singing
out of his mouth, flooding his ears and eyes,
bloomed in his voice. Eurydice had blossomed
into that landscape, out of the shadows by music:
her cheek had reddened, eye had glistened again,
brighter at every note. Her flowing shroud
unraveled as her blood ran to his song.
    Singing Eurydice, Eurydice,
    I brought her all that way to breath itself,
    beyond that kingdom—even beyond my song,
    where, for a moment, again, the sun could glimpse her.
But Orpheus—turning around, away from his strains,
for only a moment—seeing the sun again,
the miracle possible and amazing, turned
back to look as if his eyes were needed;
when all the world was watching, fixed in wonder,
wondered, himself, and turned out of his singing,
and time rumbled and turned again on its axis
to spin Eurydice out into silence and haze.
    "Farewell," she called, vanishing to air,
    and I called into empty air, "Farewell."
    And now, full of grief, I sing how it was possible

and rooted trees have been moved to hear my lament.
Angered Apollo repaired and silenced the corpse
whose head stayed tides at the flood in boundless singing,
but afterwards he wept for his dissonant son,
bereft of the world, and out of all its order,
the shining Orpheus, returned to the gray land
where music is enough. He drank of Lethe
who once had sung, in a river that could not hold him,
and loud into the ears of the sleepy world.

JERICHO

"You could see the river from camp; you could climb a tree
or stand on a high rock and stare at it
and beyond to the valley and hills that stretched west
until your eyes swam—not from emotion
but with an unblinking dumbness, for this was the end
of all the pitching and breaking of camp, of marching,
of praying, of making up songs. You do not believe
in the column of fire, of course, or the column of cloud,
but these are ways of describing the kind of faith
we all had, and you who were not there
must imagine in these unlikely ways the feeling
of high purpose, the sense of history, the pride
that the old man could breathe into us again
and again even for forty years.
                              At the end,
in sight of the river, everything fell apart,
and all of us felt old and acted young,
and the camp was a mess, and there were fights and more fights.
One man got his eyes put out, and another
got his foot chopped off with a cleaver and bled to death.
The generals issued orders, of course, and priests
summoned us for sermons and for prayers,
but there was an epidemic of dysentery
and there was all the talk that the old man
was going to die, that he had said himself
he never expected to make it across the river,
which, as I said, you could see from where we were.
So the orders and the sermons all went for nothing,

258

and at night the men would go off to Shittim and the whores.
We waited there in the spring rains and the mud
that showed our footprints, aimless as kept cattle,
until the news came back from the mountain to camp
that Moses was dead, and the soldiers wept and the women
were quiet; I remember the trite sound
of the shouting of children playing at some game
in the thin sunshine.
              I thought, 'This is the end,'
and even felt relief, as at a play
whose ending I could see and appreciate,
applauding the splendid spirit of the venture,
savoring ironies in its near-success.
There was a rightness to it which I sucked at
as at the sweetness of a decaying tooth,
all through the prayers and eulogies for Moses,
and through the following morning when I was called
to report for orders. They sent us across the river,
two of us—me and Isaacson—as spies.

There was a time I wept for Jericho,
the odd streets, loud with the cries of hawkers,
the smells of cooking, even those famous walls
which were touched with pink at sunset and then turned gray
with shadows from the turrets black as velvet.
Later, after moonrise, silvered shapes,
huger than clouds, they rode the plain.
                  I wept
for those walls once, and for the people in them
dead because it was somehow inconvenient

that the city was where it was, and that our plans
made no allowance for the fact of their existence.
But I have outgrown that old rage. Killing
is easy, is nothing. How simple it would be
to kill a man—for profit, say—and be done with it,
run your sword through his belly: you could repent
and lead an exemplary life, and be saved or damned.
But we were the chosen people, and God's will
was the dirty business we acted out
and feeling free all the time—as free as the birds
that fly, chirping and singing, north and south
spring and fall, stupid and automatic.
We entered the city at night, dressed as shepherds.
The streets smelled of manure, shops were still open
and I remember a bracelet set with garnets
that I admired. And in the taverns laughter,
talk of the day's prices, stories, complaints.
We walked the streets, cautious at first, then glad
just to be in a city.

                    At the change of the watch
we went to a whorehouse, sat with the clerks, the soldiers,
a couple of old merchants, a few farmers,
and heard the talk, which was of Israel,
the kingdoms we had conquered, and the sea
that opened for us, and then closed, drowning them.
Even the girls were afraid, standing together
at one end of the room, talking of rapes
they thought we had committed. Now and then,
one would pass among us, stroking hair,

sitting on a lap or smiling, trying
to drum up business while there was time, hoping
the talk of disaster might loosen purses, wanting
to die, if she had to die, at least with some money.
To celebrate these signs of our power, proud,
we obliged, and went up with Rachab, to her room.
Naked, she looked at us naked, and melted with terror
to see that we were circumcised, were Jews,
were part of the army of Israelites. She became
suddenly a different kind of woman,
who would not take our money, who made love
helplessly, who trembled throughout, afraid
not of what we might do but of who we were,
and later, begged for her life.
                                        One of the maids
had also seen us, had found us out, had reported
to one of her soldier friends who came with guards,
but Rachab hid us up on the roof, and lied
boldly to the soldiers, asking only
that we spare her life when we came to take the city.
Remember, we two were the first of all Israel
they had seen in the promised land. And Rachab's awe
I felt, myself, but later. And her fear.
Then I despised her as simply a traitorous whore,
which I suppose she was, but that whore's couch
was as good an altar as any I have seen
to the power of God. Never mind blessing Him,
keeping His laws, praying, but understand
that He gave us a country, and that He took it away
from the people who lived there, as a capricious cat

might keep its tit from a kitten and let it starve.
Believe in the world only, and in fortune,
and follow good luck, and pay respect to money
and this is recognition of the Lord
and reverence for His works. And of course, whoring.
We exchanged protection, and she helped us escape,
and we fled to the hills northward where we hid
while she, I suppose, went about her business,
taking on clerks and soldiers and fat merchants
and waiting for our return and her city's fall.
After three days, we made it back to camp,
gave our report, and were commended for it,
and the rest you know—how we attacked the city,
blew our horns, and saw the walls fall down.
The whole ridiculous story . . .

                    Gambling men
in a like fashion throw their chip on the cloth
and win with their eyes closed to show the world
that their luck is running, and the croupier
pays just the same, and sensible men at the table
shrug their shoulders and place their bets with the winner,
riding his luck. So Rachab was saved,
was accepted into our tribe, and we went on
to conquer the people of 'Ai, and all the land
that God promised us.

          At Jericho
we stood before the walls with those silly trumpets,
and that same year, far to the northwest,
barbarians stood before Troy (I hear with a horse)
and they too won a victory, and made up

262

their own absurd story—which is right,
and the only way to explain an absurd thing.

The land is ours now, and I plow my field,
but the terror I saw in the eyes of that girl is mine,
for the way we won was not any human way,
and I do not pee in running streams, I avoid
hunchbacks, I put on my left shoe first.
We stand here on our little eminence
and study to construe God's subtle laws,
but the column of cloud was thunder visible,
and the column of fire was obvious enough.
A row of sunflowers stands on the edge of my field,
and I watch them watch the sun, turning to westward
as the sun turns, and I have often wondered
whether the flower hates the thing it thrives on,
indifferently burning down life and decay.
Still, we could not have ignored those holy tokens
back in the desert, or found our way by ourselves."

THREE ADAPTATIONS FROM CATULLUS

Comely Contumely (lxxxiii)
Lesbia insults me in front of her spouse,
and he's delighted, laughs, brays like a mule?
A lot he knows! She plays at cat-and-mouse.
(But who is which? Who's watching at the hole?)

If she'd forgot me, if her lovely wound
had healed, there'd be no snarling, no attack.
But she remembers. Let her rage resound.
It is a call to arms. She will be back.

A Funny Thing Happened on the Way to the Forum (lvi)
Cheer up, Cato, your fine funk
is catching. Laughter's the prune
for cramped minds. There was a punk
I came on this afternoon . . .

Quite so. You complain of our lives. You long
for justice? Listen! This kid
was humping Matilda (lovely song!)
and for you, here's what I did . . .

(For your sake, and for justice's,
for turnabout is fair.)
I turned him about and thrust, as is
my constant pride and care.

Terrible buggers we are, and knaves.
But perhaps we were meant to be.
So let them mark upon our graves:
"They were tools of divinity."

The Breath of Scandal, for Victius (xcviii)
From licking assholes—and their boots—
your tongue has grown strong, old boy.
Your words don't even matter, toots;
your exhalations can destroy.

PETER DE LUNA

Peter de Luna (*benedicite!*)
became at Avignon Pope Benedict,
thirteenth of that name.

     Berry was for him;
Burgundy, Orleans, and the others waited;
Brittany followed the King, waiting, waiting . . .
perhaps to hear from Clement in Rome.

"To say the truth"
     (What else would Froissart say?)
"he was a devout man and of a contemplative life."
But, my God!
    Le Pappe de la Lune?

The schism continued. When has there not been schism?
In my lifetime, my father's, or his father's?
It was said that the gates of Paradise had shut
and not a single soul had entered in
for fifty years.
    Five hundred now, gentles.
Peter de Luna, captive at Avignon,
vowed not to clip his beard till he was freed.
The Vow of the Heron (q.v.) —
      and still the heron
flies across the sky in the afternoons;
at night clouds beard the moon. Peter's beard.
He waits to be freed? Or is it the other Peter,
asleep at the rusted gates?

266

EPITAPH FOR GOLIATH

After so many victories, one
defeat, and that one by a stone:
but let this stone atone for that
breach of the order of combat.
He was a victim of a ruse
of the rude boy of the barbarous Jews.
Goliath shall have honor while
men yet have any use for style
or the purity of form they mean
by the accolade of Philistine.

DIALOGUE IN ITHAKA

"Those impossible tales he tells Penelope . . ."
    "She believes him."
"And her story of the years she spent weaving . . ."
    "He believes her."
"You really think that they believe each other?"
    "Man, you'll believe anything!"

SAPPHIC FRAGMENTS

Because of my pain she wrote.
The rest is gone.
Editors, blinder than Homer, fire,
water, rot, monks, the rotten
bishop, St. Gregory of Nazi
                              anzos,
mummy wrappers, perverse, preserved
only this. Imagine
                    Because of
Achilles' wrath . . .
                    Imagine the rest.
Her silence, the silence of women, fascinates.
It and her *Garlands of celery* make
a mad scene, an entire *Hamlet* but
with men left out—Queen Gertrude and Ophelia.
"We shall give," said the father could be her *Lear.*
But what of *As long as you wish?*
Who speaks, who sacrifices herself, and suffers until
Unexpectedly?
Everything is.
Even *The queenly dawn.* Everything
is unexpectedly because of her pain.

BELISARIUS

At last Belisarius, cleared of the charge of treason,
regained his titles, had his wealth returned,
and eight months later died, honorably.
And if Justinian confiscated then
most of the estate, it was no insult.
The emperor often confiscated estates,
and the widow was left with something, and of course,
the affair had been embarrassing, after all.

That "Give a penny to Belisarius"
is only a fiction of John Tzetzes, monk
and sentimentalist. The general
was not blinded, never had to beg,
never said any such thing.
                              But the tale endures
because it is horrible and not surprising,
and, having saved the city from the Bulgars,
having been great, he ought to have come to begging.

One does develop a taste for this grinding down.

A VICTORY FOR THE EASTERN EMPIRE

Eastward beyond the Oxus, Yezdegerd,
grandson of Chosroes and the last
Sassanian king of Persia, fled the sword,
Khalid, and the Moslems, seeking the aid
of Li Shih-min who was the T'ang T'ai Tsung,
acknowledged master of forty-four Tartar hordes,
to recover the leathern apron, the gold cuirass,
the fire that had burned twelve hundred years.

Beyond the Jaxartes, at Scythia, he proclaimed
his friendship with the T'ang, the interest of China,
and raised a Turkish army to retake Persia.
They turned against him, too. At a small stream,
he begged a miller with a little boat
to leave his milling for the afternoon
and row his king across. The haggling.
The offer of bracelets, refused. The demand for silver.
And Yezdegerd slew this miller. His son, Firuz,
shoved off in the boat, and the Turks came.
And Firuz, at the far bank, was an orphan.

He made his way along the Tarim River,
called there Hsi Yu, across the Shen Shen desert
and into Han and the capital, Ch'ang An.
And lived in Ch'ang An, as the King of Persia,
acknowledged thus by all, under T'ang T'ai Tsung,
and into the reign of Kao and the Empress Wu.

And Firuz named his son Ni-Ni-Shih.

COLLOQUY BETWEEN TWO KINGS

Having met grief with honor, they are great—
even literally, for we sense their size
more than we hear their words at the city gate:
the stranger who has daughters for his eyes
offers protection to Athens out of his hate,
and Theseus listens and shows no surprise.

That two, whom the world has used so, should confront
one another, observe amenities, stand
on the same ground, would seem an outrageous stunt
some eager, tactless press agent had planned,
except that they only indirectly allude
to the signatures of intolerable grief:
the color of a sail, a fork in the road.
Their manners are what burden our belief.

ST. EBBA OF COLDINGHAM

Abbess Ebba feared the Danes,
pirates come to roister,
plunder, loot, and—surely—rape
the sisters of the cloister.

Clever Ebba took a razor
in her most pious grip,
cut off her nose, and then, to make sure,
sliced off her upper lip.

Then, in the hall of the chapter house,
with blood splotched on her wimple,
she explained, appealed to the rest of the nuns,
who followed her example.

The dreaded pirates came and saw
the mutilated gape
of all those faces cut to spite
the awful fate of rape.

Perhaps in disappointment, or
perhaps in disgust, the Danes
considered Ebba's abbey and
the extraordinary pains

the nuns had taken to frustrate
their casual desire,
and set alight the abbey, burning
all to their death in fire.

Ebba earned a sainthood and
the pirates put to sea,
amazed at a God, a faith more cruel
than pirates could think to be.

JONAH: A REPORT

He is mad. He is filthy. He sits all day in his shack.
He says he never sleeps and never wakes,
but hangs between in a trance. His hair is white
and yet we know his age is thirty-one.
The cures are remarkable. Of course, the doctors
say he is a fake, but cannot explain
the cases, scores of them, hundreds, of small children
sick to death with fever and brought to him
at the last moment, when all other hope is lost,
and suddenly well again. And deaf made to hear
and blind to see again. The usual things.

The dream, however, is dangerous. He says
that all his powers came to him in the dream,
and he tells the dream, over and over again.
We have asked him, we have begged him to desist,
but still he tells his dream, this blasphemous dream,
which threatens our religion and our people.

The Dream
"I lay three days. The coffinmaker came
to make my coffin, but while he worked the wood,
I heard my sickness speak to me. It promised
that from the Lord of the Ocean I might receive
the gift of healing. Therefore I asked my father
to let my body be buried at once, in the sea.

  "They carried me to the harbor and found a ship
ready to set sail, and loaded me on.
My sickness churned the sea, and the mariners

threw me over the side and sailed away.
I fell upon the ocean in my coffin,
and the coffin was a boat which bore me, swifter
than any ship. I came, then, to an island
where the Lady of the Ocean makes her home.
Naked, she welcomed me, and gave me her teat
and suckled me, and sang to me of hardships,
of the trouble I should find, and the weariness.
I laid my head in her lap and slept awhile.

    "When I woke, alone, to the rushing of wings,
I saw a bird like an eagle, but larger, larger,
with feathers of iron and beak of blackest stone.
The eagle plucked me up and carried me
to the top of a mountain. There a birch tree grew,
and the Lord of the Tree bade me break a branch,
but when I touched the tree, it groaned and cried.
I broke a twig, the smallest I could find,
and felt the pain of it in my little finger,
which also broke, but when I touched the twig
to the broken finger, it healed me instantly.
The Lord of the Tree approved and told me his secrets,
the seven virtues of the seven plants,
the powers of nine stones and of nine metals.

    "I visited the tents of illness, torn,
and in a barren place. In the first tent, Syphilis
tore out my living heart. In the next, Madness
cut off my head. Leprosy peeled my skin,
and the others took my nerves, my bones, my blood.
But the eagle, who is Lord of the Sky, returned
and carried my body's pieces to a cave

where a smith with one eye beat upon an anvil
and forged me whole again. I was molten hot
and he threw me down to cool in a deep pool.
    "The pool was a part of the ocean, very deep
where all the oceans meet. The Lord of the Ocean
sulks there, in his castle. He was the Lord
of Chaos before our God created the world
and separated dry land from the water.
The Lord of the Ocean is angry, and sends the waves
to beat upon the land to wash it away,
and sends the storms to sink the ships of land
that sail upon his sea, and sends the wind
to blow down trees that men build into ships.
He fought with me and killed me many times,
but every time I lived again, and was stronger,
for the smith had forged me well. The Lord of the Ocean
at last relented and offered me his daughter,
an ugly hag with green snakes for her hair,
scales for skin, sea scallops for her dugs.
I lay with her (and still I stink of fish)
and she told me her father's secrets—of the waters,
fresh and salt, and all the sacred springs,
and how to find the water when digging wells.
Then she put me inside an enormous fish
which brought me back to earth and Nineveh."

He does not insist, of course, on the literal truth
of everything in the dream, but he does repeat it,
and the people, because he cures their children, believe.
The man is remarkable, but Israel

cannot survive his kindnesses. Therefore,
the committee on heterodoxy recommends
that Jonah be stoned to death, as the law prescribes,
but privately, and at night. In a few years
if he is not forgotten, let us publish
our own, official account of his exploits.
We can make him a minor prophet, let him go
on a voyage, even let him get thrown in the sea,
and on his return he can preach something inoffensive—
virtue and reform are the usual things.
This is our report and our proposal,
submitted on the fifteenth day of Adar,
in the year 3436 of the Lord's people.

PROLOGUE TO A PLAY: SAMUEL SPEAKS

The miraculous days are over. Now there is no
belief or disbelief but something halfway,
halfhearted. The conscript army parades and the people
cheer, but it is a vain hope and has no object.
They wait for another miracle, but have forgotten
what they are waiting for, that they wait at all.
Even the very old can hardly remember
stories they heard in childhood: of crossing the desert,
water gushing from the struck rock, food
falling from the sky, the sea parting.
Not even the children now accept such tales.
The state therefore was necessary for endurance,
the freshness of love having somehow run dry.
And now will a man love his wife by the state's contract
and father will feed his son by the state's law,
and widow will have the farm by law, for we
who lived freely in our Father's house have demanded
a lease to our own room as between strangers.
By politics do all men become strangers,
to be dealt with as strangers. With the state will no man feed
the wanderer, with the state will no man repair
the road in front of his house. With the state no man
will teach his own child, for the state will do, compel
these things as if no virtue were in the world.
Not to the horizon, but the boundary,
not to the hilltop but the flag will men look,
and the king will rule as if there were no God.
And love with nothing to do will be sentiment,

and God with nothing to do will be an idea.
This, and more, I said, but the soul's cowardice,
which is fear of anarchy, could not be driven out.
The people demanded, and, therefore, I anointed
Saul, a common man, and made him king.

WORDSWORTH'S MUSIC

Kick Miss Barrett's Flush and throw Hood's Dash
a peppered hamburg. Or, no, it wasn't the dogs,
which may have been decent animals, but the poets
misnaming them. Cowper's Beau was less bad.
Byron's Boatswain? A little whimsical.
Pope's Bounce was fine, and Landor's Pomero
and Giallo difficult, which is about right.
And Arnold's Geist was perfectly typical
(and somewhat redeemed by the breed—it was a dachshund).
But the best, I think, was Wordsworth's old bitch, Music.
Forget the poems, the sentiment, the public
gooping, and think of the name itself—Music.
Awful, all airy-fairy, unless we allow
the man a sense of humor, a sense of himself
as also animal. Figure the dog howled
to flute or fiddle, that weird falsetto yawrp,
and the name begins to be appealing, or, better,
give him a real break and let the dog
be flatulent, and Music hath charms. What poet
can keep from occasional mocking of what he does,
knowing that he is a singing tub of guts,
a rare mixed-grill, a creature—like that dog?
We keep dogs, most of us, because they teach us
how to be physical and still content,
chase rabbits, lie by the fire, and grow old
and deaf as Music got to be, and blind
so that she fell in a well at Gallow Hill
and drowned. And her master, William Wordsworth, cried—

or that's what the poem says, and I can believe it,
for it's a hard lesson we try to learn
going to the dogs, and study makes it
only harder. But Wordsworth started well
when he named the dog . . .
                              A joke it was at first,
but like all good jokes true, and maybe he heard
in that dog's passing wind a kind of music.

ART OF TORTURE

An art of torture? Ah, in the Japanese
gardens of pain, the little bonsai trees,
stunted for years, suffer to delight
with tiny gnarls and twists the recondite
tastes of the civilized. And in the West,
dog fanciers for the same long years invest
their care on a sturdy breed to miniaturize
to the charms of helplessness—all nerves and eyes—
their pets, prized, mutilated, and reduced
to elegance, like Byron, Pope, or Proust.

No thank you. Only nobody gets to pick.
Even accountants suffer, and dentists get sick
who write, compose, paint nothing whatever,
while poets—some—remain happy, trivial, clever,
knowing they have insurance, if times go bad
(the best of us, this century, were mad).

In circuses, they train young bears with heat
and make them perform, dance with their painful feet
on sizzling floors. I guess, when it happens to you,
it's handy if you can dance a step or two
and make an art of torture, crazy, juiced,
or tripping high, like Byron, Pope, or Proust.

SWOBODA

Wilhelm Kuhe "remembers that as a boy in Prague he met Wenzel Swoboda, a double bass player, who had been a member of the orchestra on the first night of Don Giovanni *in 1787, conducted by Mozart himself."*

—PROGRAM NOTES TO *La Traviata*

Kuhe reports that Swoboda remembers . . .
but what could he remember? I have been
serif to the ELI's L, have marched,
strapped to the big, blue bulldog's thoompa-thoom,
and have heard the fweedle of the clarinets
dribbling down my ears. The trumpets' tune
was yards away, fluttering the flags
at the end of the bowl. We marched down the field
as letters we could not read, were ourselves the words.
And Swoboda heard nothing, and saw nothing,
remembered nothing but that his bow had moved
with a baton as twigs of the same tree
moving in a wind. What was there to tell
but his double bass's zormm-zormm-zormm?

LEPORELLO, IN HIS DRESSING ROOM

Il padron mio . . . but we never spoke Italian
or sang in Salzburger harmonies. Don Juan
was Spanish, after all, a petty grandee
with a sallow complexion, too much grease in his hair,
and fatter than you'd imagine. His voice was deep,
not the rich basso you hear in your mind's ear,
but deep enough to be attractive to women—
many, but not that many. That thousand and three
he had in Spain couldn't have been six hundred,
which is still a lot, but beside the point. The numbers
are inflated because they are easy to understand.
He is remembered, but why he is remembered
has been forgotten. They make up all kinds of stories,
intricate seductions, changes of costume,
me, the lowly Leporello, singing
under the balcony to his direction,
which is closer, having to do with the style of the thing
but not yet it, not him, not what I remember.
Think of the end, the dead *commendatore*,
the statue come to dinner. God, I was scared,
and he was, too. He was. I could see him tremble,
but he would not repent, would not, wrenched himself loose
and lay on the floor, quivering in fear,
and still would not take any of it back.
You hear the shriek, which is neither Italian nor Spanish,
nor any other language, nor even music
except for the instruments running down the scale,
a pure shriek, as the devils carry him off,

and it stays with you in the taxi, all the way home.
It has stayed with me for years, in my ear, throat,
and I understand it: the cry of the faithful servant,
for he was a servant too, his own man,
serving his pleasure as I was serving him.
But he was more loyal than I, or any man,
and would not betray at the end that little master,
nor lose his honor just to keep his soul.

THE DEATH OF MOZART

Uraemia is painful enough without birds
chirping their heads off, warbling in thirds
while you're busy dying. A little quiet, please.
I want no canary around for my decease.
No more did he. But still, it is bothersome
to think that when his final hour had come
Mozart sent his canary away. Did the bird
make mistakes? sing badly what Mozart heard
in his mind's ear, following a score
of canary music? Or, did the bird soar
on aviary arias, a strain
so fine that he beat time with throbs of pain?
Or worse, did the bird's song suggest a measure
there was no more time for, now, so that the pleasure
of composing turned to the pain of holding a flood,
as the body held the urine in the blood?
I fear the worst, that Mozart, as you or I,
just wanted quiet, quiet in which to die,
unbroken by any sound but his own breath.
With the bird gone, he had quiet. Which was death.

HOMAGE TO LUIGI BOCCHERINI

1.

Landon to Haydn's Roosevelt, Luigi
Boccherini also ran
                          bows over strings
made minor music poor (I mean unmoneyed)
and died poor.

Melody, child of a pennywhistle mind,
brings out the warbler in us, chirruping sparrow,
the color of jays, gay and gliding:
all laud and honor then from the dancing dons
that whistle across the court, and pay ye all homage
to Boccherini and his singing like.

Not the common man; not great, nor near great,
nor "for trying" but *ipse*, good as he was,
musician, music (i.e. of the muse),
and in that thrall—like to a priesthood,

                                    like to a disease . . .
That mind could pulse the heartbeat, fleshed and ringing,
praise Boccherini, awful and abstract.

2.

I have heard that agile playing
in drowsy claret afternoons,
poised upon some fragile word
of mine, or drifting on his tunes,
and loved as he was close to me
and trembled at his violin.

Boccherini, peerless, plays
the dancing shadows' coming in.

3.

"Poet, make up your miracles, work your wonders:
that epic sop: tell him your blood is his:
journey: blind, crazy, clubfoot, or drunk:
harrow again, or climb the mountain and ask

What world is this of yours? what thing this music?

and make him speak as you have found him out."

But intervals of voices in the hearing,
in the world's hearing, faint as they were, are
(as, say, a small saint's obscure passion)
                                        his
and done for the doing, favor or heaven, or no.
Then let him alone, you; he could give over
this and the next world, and without such questions,

and as you fear his music, fear him, praise
and, silent, hallow Boccherini, dead.

MUSICIAN AT COURT

The infanta's dreams reigned, in some other kingdom,
while he played sonatas upon a gilt harpsichord,
not paying attention, like her, in a private thralldom.
The courtiers were even perceptibly bored.
The infanta, at moments, would listen to what she heard,
raising an eye or a fingertip, and he
would repeat the passage without saying a word,
nod—not to her, but to rhythm—and would reflect
on matters of counterpoint and polyphony,
and how disparate themes will sometimes intersect.

SERMONETTE

Nigel Bruce, as Watson, sings
"Loch Lomond," and surprisingly well,
  in *Pursuit to Algiers*. I know these things
are nonsense, of course, and yet they compel

our tatters of attention. The tune
comes after Rathbone recalls the gifts
of Moriarty on the bassoon.
(Holmes is a violinist.) It shifts,

and Cavett gets Ustinov to tell
how he'd preferred the bassoon, but found
flutes in demand at school . . . Oh, well!
And he imitates the flautist's sound

in a *trompe d'oreille*, the way he did cars
on that record of the Gibraltar Grand Prix.
A commercial: a woman performs a few bars
of "Seventy-six Trombones" on the free

goblets you can get with eight
gallons or more of Union gas.
The offer is limited. It's late,
and I turn it off. But upon the glass

of my mind's tube, there's still a jumble.
The Prince of Ruvenia's on his way!
Art should be proud; oil should be humble.
Sherlock Holmes should not have to say

that talents are never guarantees
of character. That was Arnold's view,

but the violin Mephistopheles
(and Holmes) used to play is now a kazoo.

"Gentlemen, in the interests of
democracy, I accept the case."
Thank you, Rathbone, and Ustinov,
and Cavett, for putting a cheerful face

on the bad news. I know how it is:
If love is never having to say
you're sorry, democracy (gee whiz!)
is having nothing left to betray.

ADAPTATIONS FROM THE SWABIAN

1.

Ludovici is become ambitious.
Having spent years buggering chickens, turkeys,
geese, and ducks, in a congenial barnyard,
he now sports a new jerkin, new leather boots,
and looks longingly at the mountaintop,
lusting, no doubt, after eagles.

2.

The playful matchmakers have spoken to the bishop
of the charms of Xenia, and told her of his interest.
Perhaps they will meet some evening. Perhaps not.
But in the cafes, it is all the talk now:
imagine the union of two such flatulent persons.

3.

Horst is in jail for attempted bribery.
His offer was so small as to be insulting
to the alderman who, therefore, had no choice
but to punish Horst for criminal stinginess.

4.

When Arpad goes to the brothel
he gets a discount, which is only fair,
considering the small size of Arpad's doodle.

5.

Deaf and blind, he was nearly perfect for Hulda,
but he refused her, too. And what a shame!
If only they had thought to cut off his nose.

6.

Zoltan was seen, leaving the bookseller's stall.
Such pretentiousness—to announce to the town
he is too good to wipe his bum with leaves.

FROM THE NOTEBOOKS OF DA VINCI

Leonardo puzzled: how to put
a round dome on a square building.
All solutions cheat; some more graceful,
some sly, others crude and bold, none
satisfactory.
     It figures,
as the round horizon over our right rectangles—
acres, hectares, plots and plats,
convenient squares with which we grid the globe—
all intellectual life, the circles of spirit
impeaching the sensible squares, form fighting form
(spirit and mind, say: any such pair
of contradictory truths).
     So Leonardo
scribbled in his notebook, sketched and scratched . . .
It couldn't be done. The square peg would not,
will not fit in the round hole. It will not
melt away by artifice, behave
plausibly.
     The Renaissance was wrong,
a retarded child, sweating the I.Q. test,
knuckles white with effort, the peg and hole
stupider than he.
     Frustration flings
the test away. Only the worst keep working,
persevere, push, puzzling.

Hopeful?
                    Hopeless:
trying here to design that impossible duomo
that can only be built—if at all—in the City of God.

PROLEGOMENON TO THE STUDY OF POETICS

The population doubles itself and redoubles.
We are squeezing out the animals; the time will come
when we squeeze out one another. Minerals wash
into the oceans; the Atlantic and the Pacific
get to be more and more like the Dead Sea.
I understand the moon is getting closer,
will fall back, will kill us all one day.
I hear the clock tick and wait for silence.

Oh, but the poems! What about the poems?

The Greeks, the Jews, the Chinese have misled us.
Think, rather, of some exquisite Mayan
or of an Etruscan bard, or of all the minstrels
of cultures you and I have never heard of . . .
Try to imagine their intricate lyrics, praising
the beauty of the moon, of the sea, of love.

IMPROVISATION ON THEMES OF JOHN DONNE

We know that keening. What we do not know
is whether the comptroller is in a hurry, or Otto
Preminger is passing through, or the cops
are speeding after a speeding driver, or before
an ambulance, for a birth or a death. It stops

but we do not send to know for whom the siren
screams. It will be in the papers, tucked in with the foreign
exchange listings and port departures. It's not,
anyway, for us, except to wonder whether
it's car or driver or fire itself that's hot.

Those horsemen ride in style now—Cadillacs—
ambulances and hearses; or fire trucks
by La France with the silver siren on the side.
Death is proud, an official who sometimes deigns
to take a lucky constituent for a ride.

VARIATIONS ON AN ANCIENT THEME

Fellah farms while frigatoon
ferries fangots featly;
I fetch my feeze for the farandole
and the end of fending
at the nightfall.

Unbraced, unpinned, unbreeched, unbound,
the moon unblemished rises,
unsays ukase of urgent day,
restores *Ursprache*
usquebaugh's way.

Cumbent creatures rouse to cruise,
crave cock-a-hoop consortium:
caliph carousers, caitiff canoodlers,
they pair and creep
to their cozy croodlers.

Kakapo cries and kea gorges
on the kidney fat of sheep.
In a kajawah my love comes
across the karroo
and the kanoon thrums.

A SHORT TROT WITH UCCELLO'S HORSES

Sir John de Hawkwood rides a sea-green horse
on a field plum-purple, up on the north wall
of this "somewhat bare and chilly" duomo, echo
of the deeper green outside of the Prato marble
or simply a kind of cinquecento whimsey . . .
this pistachio prancing.

                         Friars ride their Vespas,
their rope ceintures whipping the wind, and women
in broughams to Ferragamo's nibble *gelati:*
for Sir John, why not a light lime-phosphate horse?
But in the Uffizi, Uccello's sketch omits
any rider at all, and upstairs in Battaglia
(and in Paris, Bataille; in London, Battle) horses
of the same feather trample the true enough gore,
but smiling with carousel glee.

                           They are not monsters,
do not have heads of tigers, wings of birds,
or tails of vipers seven times coiled. Sir John,
on a green griffon, a yellow yale, could ride
whatever walls he would, and with surer seat
than on this horse that is not a horse, this beast
that is no beast.

                Over a Strega with ice
that night in the Piazza della Signoria
you said, "The odd thing in the way the city looks
is its natural feeling of power. That homey fort,"
you said, and nodded toward the Palazzo. Horses
are also tame, and those old condottieri

rode them unthinking, as polo players can;
but a green horse that is no horse, those grinning
beasts in Uccello's canvases, whose riders
are irrelevant holders of spears, fountains of blood,
are deceptive as power, as wild, as giddy, as green.

DA VINCI SUNSET

Michelangelo's paint pots and Raphael's cartoons
weary the master. Tired of pictures, he spends his afternoons
discussing mirrors with the Germans,
arguing optics and light,
or experimenting with varnishes to get the formula right.
    Leonardo has become
    intrigued by a grander medium.

For the Holy Father's datary, he has done a Madonna and Child.
The picture, he said, was nothing, but the pigments, he said, were
    wild.
And now he is making a lizard
into a dragon with wings.
He has fashioned horns and a beard for it: his art form now is things.
    Leonardo has become
    intrigued by a grander medium.

The wings are constructed of lizard scales, by quicksilver attached
to the back of his lizard dragon. He has said to those who have
    watched:
"Buonarroti, flat on his back,
could lie for a thousand years,
but before those fingers move to meet, my dragon will wiggle his ears."
    Leonardo has become
    intrigued by a grander medium.

Now he is making animals of a wax of a certain kind
and by shaping them thin and hollow and filling them with wind
he makes them fly around the room.

He is crazy, people say.
He calls Pygmalion fool and says all pictures are child's play.
Leonardo has become
intrigued by a grander medium.

RIDE THE HIGH COUNTRY

1.

The long red underwear of Randolph Scott,
the gold-rimmed spectacles of Joel McCrea,
underscore age, and through the reverend plot
the old gunfighters ride for one more day.

And Ladd was old in *Shane,* and in *High Noon*
old Coop had all his wrinkles emphasized
(with visible distaste he drew his gun).
The ritual of honor is disguised

and is an act of memory and will.
The pistol-packing, popcorn-eating child
feels the pretended stubble on his chin
and imagines his bones weary after the kill.
Even the movies' West is no longer wild,
its *virtu* now a trail bum, a has-been.

2.

Odysseus, safe at home, can be our friend.
Orestes and the Furies come to terms
—our terms: we, craven, crave the tamest end,
the fireside remembrances of storms,

the hero's diminution. The old hand
is slower on the draw, the eyes are gone.
We may admire, but we understand
that nerve is all McCrea is working on,

that aged manliness becomes absurd.
He makes mistakes out on the trail, he has

fallen into their obvious trap, is hit,
and crumples with gun blazing. On the hard
ground he shakes our comfort as he dies,
affirming the agelessness of what is fit.

FINANCIAL STATEMENT

Benjamin Franklin, egomaniac, lecher,
a penny saved is a penury earned. Your eye
upon this donut, brother: "Fresh Tuesday"
but bought on Wednesday. It is a meek new world,
the saving of six cents an exercise
of the soul. The hair of heroes, the hair of angels,
and angels' harps are all the color of money,
and heaven shines like a bank vault, but copper is hell
and the deepest pit is the penny black from holding,
coin of the common people, Lincoln's friends,
slaves still.
             The taste is nearly the same.
But when it came back from the waters, all ninefold,
it was not day-old 27¢
as are these donuts,

                    which were a deliberate choosing.
The finitude grows like a fungus. Destitute Dick,
does your almanack tell me where is fancy bread?

I think of my infant daughter's ravening
and know what Adam hoped against all knowledge:
that somehow his sons would escape to have their fill
of all the best that he had had until
that marked-down, day-old apple ended it.

306

MEDITATION

"We are," he said, "more saintly than Francis, for we
lecture to stones," and we laughed, and I thought of the stones
and rocks he had meant, of Shakespeare, and I thought
of those others *Bleste be ye man yt spares thes stones*
and wondered what's in a stone.
                              We long for them
for they are long in time and longer than wonder
that the child feels finding one sudden morning
when he has learned to reckon that this clock
and that chair, say, and all those spoons
are older than he and know the prior world
where he was not.
                  Amazing as the rattle
of his growing, sucked and stared at, held or flung,
is this his ageing to knowledge of age. And stones
are old, standing in graveyards, grayer than brains,
and we are as silent with them as he with pebbles
held in a pink hand feeling them hard.
He clicks them together, throws them far, far, far . . .
who will think, awake, in a sweet goodnighted room
of the safe, dumb stone, under a bush
and be sad.
        He:I.
                And envious
because it is smooth or round or rough or shaped,
but hard, harder than any head that knows it.
I have heard tell of the painter's fear of canvas,
bare and stupid; even more the sculptor,
before that hulking silence, dreads the stone.

UPON RECEIVING A BOOK OF POEMS

For George Garrett

Your book is . . . But another friend was here
who'd brought a house gift for us, a crystal bowl,
a coincidence, but our minds work that way,
and the world, as we have agreed, is a teaching machine.
It's a lovely bowl, clean of line, clear,
and catching the light live. When he'd left the room,
I did what we all do, sooner or later,
deliberately or just by accident,
and flicked my fingernail against its rim.
It's a good bowl, and the crystal rang and rang.
The sound of the glass was clear as its light and line.
And I have read your book, and flicked my nail
against its rim, and having done so, thank you,
for the air rings, sings with a clear tone.

Never mind well-wrought urns, but consider this bowl,
and what it would be if it could never break
but go on ringing, as if God's own nail
had struck it. Books are like that sometimes. Yours is.

SESTINA FOR TEA TIME

More than the words of a conversation, the taste
sticks to the tongue, like frozen metal. The tea
we drink from these pottery cups turns the room
into some precious Swinburnian relic, the mind
adding its own flavor. Just the idea
of tea is a leaf you cannot filter out.

I think of Turgenev, his elaborate tea set out,
the sugar held in the teeth as an idea
is held in the mind (and the idea takes on the taste
of the sugar). Or I think of a blue and gold room
into some precious Swinburnian relic, the mind
of some great gentleman, as we sip tea.

And I think of the Brontës, somehow, as always at tea.
Lapsang souchong or jasmine each has its taste,
so is there a flavor to each idea
which is blended into the cup or is strained out.
This afternoon, this tea, us, this room
could become, in time, a part of the taste of the mind.

That the words will be gone is nothing, for somehow the mind
retains the faces, furniture, just as a taste.
Good talk goes with tea, and years later the tea
still tastes of that talk. It is not unlike the idea
of conversation with the words left out—
as of lovers, say, at last alone in a room.

A glass of beer at night, thus, may turn a room
into some fictive Heidelberg, where the mind
gets drunk, and the body stays sober. The taste

of Hegel, for instance, has nothing to do with tea
unless you studied him in England—out
of such irrelevant circumstances an idea

acquires physique, becomes sensible; and an idea
needs this to survive. It may live in tea
longer than in books, and come to mind
one afternoon, suddenly filling the room
when you were sure that intellect had stepped out
and you were left alone with feeling and taste.

An old friend, an idea, should have a room
where it can visit, somewhere out of the mind,
in the house of taste, perhaps, with a cup of tea.

ANOTHER LETTER TO LORD BYRON

Everyone gets junk mail, a bill, a notice
   of a private sale, an alumni fund appeal,
letters from strangers . . . The one that Auden wrote is
   one of these, though clever enough. Did you feel
the eight-krona stamp redeemed it? That's ten zlotys,
   or about a hundred lire—not a great deal,
but the names of the coins are diverting. Or possibly you
collect postage stamps? It's something to do.

It must be dull to be dead. You can't write,
   or, if you do, you can't send it off to the printer
the way you used to. So a letter might
   have been fun to get. Did you spend the winter
feeling the envelope, holding it up to the light,
   and wondering whom you knew in such a hinter-
land as Iceland? I know it would pique
my interest to get mail from Reykjavik.

Harwich is less impressive, surely, than is
   Reykjavik. But when I go to post
my letter, I may do so from Hyannis,
   which is more amusing. Or there are a host
of towns named after you. The one in Maine is
   closest, but you have a wandering ghost—
which is fitting. There's a Byron or Byronville
in Okla., Wyo., Calif., Minn., and Ill.

But never mind. The postmark's hardly crucial.
   The main thing is that after thirty years
another letter that's addressed to you shall

seem, I trust, no great intrusion. There's
lots that's happened, though I hope the news shall
    not depress you. Three decades of wars,
and the prospect of a future about which it's said
that those who are left alive will envy the dead.

But politics is not at all my métier.
    You took it up at the end, I know, but I
find it vicious enough, if rather petty (a
    moral hedging), to deal with the canaille
of publishers, editors, agents. Those *diavoletti!* (Eh?
    That's nearly impossible to justify.
But then I've just been to Venice, and saw your palazzo.
Is that enough excuse to polyglot so?)

I've changed the subject sooner than I'd intended,
    but as long as I'm on the new one, literature
is just as much a mess as ever—splendid
    livings for lousy authors, and good books fewer
and farther than ever between . . . But then, when did
    it ever appear to be better or different? You are
a perfect example of what can happen when
a poet is taken up by other men,

to be praised or damned. The public is mostly jerks.
    The common reader is common, and to hell
with him and with critics, trading in smiles and smirks,
    and making careers for themselves with their swell
Collected Essays more in mind than the works
    in hand. Even you're not doing too well.
I mention the disrepair of your reputation
only to demonstrate that of our situation.

No one reads poetry anyway now, except
    other poets—which is quite distressing.
They cannot be much as readers, being inept
    as rhymers (those that can rhyme), while confessing
to mental illness, or listing girls they've slept
    with (those that like girls) . . . But I am digressing.
In a time of tastelessness and epic slaughter,
we need some of your hock and soda water.

Not that it's all that bad. There is some verse
    well wrought. One can get in an age of iron
good iron work sometimes. A pigskin purse
    can be made of a sow's ear. One may not expire on
the beauty of it, but one could do worse.
    The manipulation of language . . . But, Lord Byron,
I scarcely need tell you. Your magnificent feminine
rhymes are more than fun for apothegming in.

They show contempt for the worst kind of good taste,
    and for readers—most of the few—who save up snatches
to make a mental sampler of, the paste
    pot minds of crackpots. And the catch is
that by the way you sneer at the whey-faced
    intellectuals who can't tell dispatches
of the AP from poems, look for meanings,
and of course miss all the point in their dull gleanings.

I hadn't meant to go on so. Do excuse
    my grumbling. I know it's rather foolish,
but I've been depressed lately. All the news
    is bad; the weather's damp and has turned coolish;
my mood's dark, the color of a bruise.

And I've been bothered by the very ghoulish
notion that the books around me may
come to life and attack me any day.

Or not the books, but their authors, all the dead
   giants of letters whom time has not quite hushed.
It'd be delightful except that they have shed
   their skins, their flesh, their bones, and are all crushed
to disembodied voices, dull as lead.
   I have the feeling that I am ambushed
by the naked ones who have shown up to haunt
me. But I can't imagine what they want.

I shouldn't like to think it's vampirism,
   nor envy, nor contempt. Perhaps they warn
that poetry is light spread through a prism,
   and suddenly, on some innocuous morn
the prism breaks, and the recidivism
   is to the whiteness from which it was born—
no rhetoric, no images, no sound,
just volumes of blank pages, buckram-bound.

Or they sing, hey-diddle, the cat and the fiddle—but
   even its nine lives prove to be finite,
and after performing on lengths of its own gut,
   it dies and the music dies. There's a moral in it.
I'm sure there is. I can't tell you just what,
   but I'm sure I'll think of something. Give me a minute.
Art is odd. Consider the dog and how
he laughed to see the hell scared out of the cow.

Well, here I am, half-dog, half-cow, half-cat
   (that's too many halves by half). All right, half-wit,

fooling around as you did once. But that
   is greatly comforting: in the little skit
from the Nightmare Follies—now in its fifth week at
   my local, mental theater—you're a big hit.
Among those shades, you shine, and my attention all
focuses on you, who are three-dimensional.

You come through whole, and live, and are not merely
   a name on the spine of your book and its index card.
The gestures you make in your poems, the jokes, are clearly
   those of a man who's trying very hard
—and willing to pay the price, even pay dearly—
   not only not to be boring, but not to be bored
himself. Yourself. Myself. I know how it is.
It's always tough in the Quality Lit. Biz.

Therefore, my letter. Partly to let you know
   that you're still alive and well, which pleases me
as much as it pleases you, and to say hello.
   With any luck, in two thousand and three,
somebody else will drop you a line, and so
   keep the game going. Auden, I, he
thank you for teaching how to play it coolly.
It is, as I am, sir, yours, very truly.

317